LIVING
BEYOND SUCCESS

Other Books by George Bockl

LIVING BEYOND SUCCESS

The Adventure of Balancing the Secular and Spiritual Aspects of Life

by GEORGE BOCKL

DEVORSS *Publications*

ISBN: 0-87516-662-8
Library of Congress Catalog Card Number: 93-72629

Printed in the United States of America.

DEDICATED TO

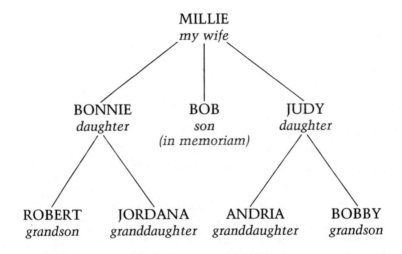

MILLIE
my wife

BONNIE
daughter

BOB
son
(in memoriam)

JUDY
daughter

ROBERT
grandson

JORDANA
granddaughter

ANDRIA
granddaughter

BOBBY
grandson

CONTENTS

Biography of an Autobiography

Living Beyond Success is a biography of an autobiography. A novel, biography, or feature article reveals less about the author than writing an autobiography, where events and emotions are not objectively researched but intimately bared to the reader.

Writers have produced sublime literature without giving a peep into their personal lives. Great works of art do not necessarily reflect their creators' character. I've seen a renowned artist wobbling in an alcoholic stupor alongside his paintings of birds that shimmered wondrously with light and life. And I've heard an arrogant, mean-spirited violinist produce inspirational music that sent tingling shivers down my spine. However, there are those whose art reflect their lives, among them Ralph Waldo Emerson and Henry Thoreau, who lived what they wrote—on the frontier of new ideas.

I'm not an artist, nor do I have any particular talent. I'm one of the millions of anonymous ordinary people—with this difference: I'm trying to cross the boundary to see what's beyond the ordinary mind.

How can a carpenter, airplane pilot, accountant, machinist —or a real-estate man like myself, without any extraordinary talents—live as excitingly as those with their gifted skills? That's the main thrust of this book.

There's a rocky barrier between ordinary and extraordinary living. It's beset with doubt and ridicule. But when an ordinary person crosses it, his mindscape of dandelions changes to roses.

How did *I* cross the barrier? I found the way when I was fifty. A slight hint: It involved "catching the wind of evolution" and riding it on the promises of the Cosmic Wisdom to take me where I wanted to go.

Lest you raise a wondering, suspicious eyebrow, let me assure you that it does not deal with theology, scholasticism, or religiosity. What I try to convey comes from hundreds of discussions with dozens of men and women from different cultures, races, and religions in many parts of the world, and from closing 20,000 real-estate deals on the firing line of action, where the bullets are live and human nature is raw.

Through the prism of present understanding, I recall my vividly stored memories of events and emotions beginning at the age of five as they unfolded in the eye of the Russian Revolution, followed by escaping into Poland, wandering for two years across the face of Europe, and arriving in America as a 12-year-old illiterate. After attending a school for foreigners, graduating from the University of Wisconsin, and suffering for years the emotional trauma of joblessness, I in desperation "backed into" real estate and built a property empire that reached beyond my wildest dreams.

The purposeful thrust of my life takes off when I dead-end into success—*and the emptiness beyond*. That's when my quest-time probings begin, challenging the barrier that divides emptiness from fulfillment.

There's an inspirational excitement to living beyond success, or any prosaic life. It lies waiting for anyone willing to cross the barrier.

I know it's there. I found it.

LIVING
BEYOND SUCCESS

1

IN THE EYE OF THE RUSSIAN REVOLUTION

*The Young Communist Lions Fed on the Old
Defenseless Peasant Zebras, and the Bandit
Vultures Picked Up the Scraps.*

M Y EARLIEST RECOLLECTION OF RUSSIA WAS
the joy of sitting alongside my grey-bearded grandfather on a wagon drawn by a lumbering horse. I
remember the pungent summer smells of horse sweat and barn
manure, and the sour brine from the barrels of beer my grandfather was hauling for a brewery along the Berezina River of
Bobruisk. I was five years old.

There was a close camaraderie between my grandfather, me,
and the horse. Every morning after watching him hitch the
horse in the barn, I would bound joyfully up to the front seat
for a glorious day of riding and chattering with the person who
most filled my empty hours with joy and security. He was my
father and grandfather—my father having been blocked from
returning to Bobruisk by the First World War after he left
for America in 1913 to earn money and come back to relieve
our poverty.

My grandfather was a big, strong, gentle man. I loved him
with a fierceness that bound me to him beyond the love for my
mother, who, because I was an only child, made me the center
of her life.

There were no kindergartens, fairy tales, or toys in my childhood—only long, wonderful days with my grandfather and his horse. Instead of schooling, I peppered him with questions about why the Berezina River froze in the winter, why horses are stronger than people, and why beer had such a strong smell. Being illiterate, he answered the best he could, but I remember marveling at his wisdom. I was his favorite grandchild. The others rarely accompanied him in his drayage work.

He was my school, amusement, and caring security. My childish happiness was interrupted only when, at my mother's insistence, I had to stay home one day a week to study Torah with the rabbi. Just as much as I liked my grandfather, I disliked the rabbi. Listening to him talk about God and Moses was drudgery compared to talking with my grandfather about why men grew old, how trees grew, and was it true that Russulkas (nymphs) snatch babies from their parents and hide them deep in the forest.

My grandfather was coughing a lot, and when I asked him why, he told me it happens to people who grow old. That satisfied me, but when he stayed home several days a week, and I missed my rides, a worry swept over me. And when he stopped working, and spent most of his days in bed, I would cry a lot—feeling sorry for him, and for myself. A sadness replaced those glorious days of riding together.

One evening he called me to his bed and, putting his hands on my head, blessed me with a few Hebrew words that I didn't understand. His voice was barely beyond a whisper. I looked into his kindly eyes and burst into tears. My world was slipping away. A man came in and asked me to leave. An hour later my grandfather died.

I couldn't sleep that night. My mind whirred with uncontrollable grief. I lost the most joyous part of my life. It would never be the same again. The despair hung over my mind for months.

✡   ✡   ✡   ✡   ✡   ✡

LIKE TEVYE IN *Fiddler on the Roof*, my grandfather was the goodwill bridge between the Jews and the potential pogromniks who, out of antisemitism or fun, especially when they got drunk, would go on a binge to beat up or kill Jews. When my grandfather died, fears of pogroms heightened.

My mother and I lived in a house with two other families. One of them had three sons: Gershon, Motte, and David, aged 17 to 21. They were part of a Jewish vigilante group who guarded Jewish homes. But at ten I was already old enough to know that the vigilantes were no match for a band of hooligans. I listened avidly to the elders' conversations about the latest pogrom victims. One of our relatives who had an ugly wound on his neck came to our house one day to tell us of his harrowing experience with three men who ransacked his home and then slashed his neck as they left. Our next-door neighbor screamed when she saw the pogromniks coming. They fired through the door and killed her.

These frightening stories numbed me with fear. When I'd get into bed I would think about dying. Would it hurt less with a bullet, a knife, or being hit over the head with a club?

Without my grandfather and without schooling, my days were filled with restless unhappiness and fear. The several hours a week I spent with the rabbi failed to allay my anxiety. I detected he was as fearful as I.

I didn't understand the political turmoil that was swirling around Bobruisk as Czarism was lurching into Communism. A facet of it that especially puzzled me was stories that parents were beginning to fear their own children more than the children used to fear their parents. I didn't understand it until 10-year-old Yankel, with whom I played occasionally, informed the communist authorities that his father hated Communism and was telling people to oppose it. His father was arrested and sent to Siberia.

"How could you do it against your own father?" I remember telling him.

"Because Communism is more important than parents. *You* stay at home, so you don't know what's going on. *I* go to a communist school where teachers are a lot wiser than parents. Why don't you come with me and see?"

I was confused but not convinced. Even if my mother were against Communism, which she was (but too afraid to talk about it), I could never hurt her, especially when she was my only security, with my father in America and my grandfather gone.

My mother eased my confusion and relieved my pogrom fears when she told me one day that we were leaving Bobruisk to live with her sister in Krevoya, a peasant village 10 miles away.

ᴠᴏᴧ   ᴠᴏᴧ   ᴠᴏᴧ   ᴠᴏᴧ   ᴠᴏᴧ   ᴠᴏᴧ

KREVOYA WAS A BUCOLIC PARADISE during peaceful times. Now the country village was threatened by young communist lions—who, hungry to practice their ideology, fed on defenseless zebra peasants—and by the vulture bandits, who picked up the scraps.

Before the Revolution took hold, I would visit Krevoya occasionally and romp through the nearby woods with my cousins and then stop to gather luscious strawberries, raspberries, and mushrooms. But the main treat came after we were exhausted and my aunt greeted us with glasses of foamy warm milk, minutes after drawing it from the cow.

Krevoya was a clearing about a mile long and two miles wide, surrounded by thick forest on all sides. Along its mile-long dirt road were ten *izbas* (straw-thatched roofed cottages) on each side, with open fields behind extending to the woods' edge. Alongside each izba was a *stopka* (a 10 × 10-foot cubicle, 2 feet aboveground and 5 feet deep, where the peasants kept their fruits, vegetables, and preserves).

My aunt Fruma and her three daughters and son, Sonia, Sosha, Chane, and Yoshka, from ages 8 to 14, were the only Jewish peasant family in Krevoya. Fruma's husband had left for America for the same reason my father did: to earn money and come back. But he too was stopped from returning home.

I left the pogrom fear behind but faced a new tension between the old and young, which was more intense in Krevoya than in Bobruisk. The peasants were wary of the young, who left the village to train for what later came to be known as the Komsomol. I didn't understand it then, but looking back, what was happening in Krevoya, Bobruisk, and throughout Russia was a raging battle between the czarist peasants who refused to bend, and the young who broke them in order to advance their new ideological careers.

I saw this battle explode in Krevoya. Yuri Volkov's son, Vladimir, left his father's farm to train for something more than remaining a peasant. To test Vladimir's loyalty to Communism, his superior entrusted him to get half the grain and cattle from the Krevoya peasants—especially from his father.

Vladimir drove into Krevoya at the head of a three-wagon caravan and three armed soldiers. He stopped at his family's izba first. When his father came out, Vladimir, dressed in a natty uniform, issued a strident order.

"We've come to take half your cattle and grain to feed the army."

A group of onlookers congregated, I among them.

"But I need it to feed my family."

"The army's more important than your family."

"But it's *your* family!"

"Enough talk! Get it!"

The soldiers drove one of the wagons to his father's barn. The peasant ran to block them. Vladimir drew his revolver.

"Out of the way or I'll kill you."

The two soldiers grabbed his father and pushed him into his house.

Cowed by the show of force, the father and the rest of the peasants yielded their grain and cattle with little protest, including my aunt who gave up her only cow and half her food.

During play with the children and discussions with the parents after the traumatic incident, I detected a mixture of anger and envy—anger among the parents against the young, and envy among the young who remained on the farm and saw one of their own wield so much power. Krevoya was divided, not between its peasants, but between parents and their children.

The tumultuous changing times brought an orgy of banditry. Since there were no police to turn to, bandits pillaged at will. Following numerous accounts of robberies and killings of defenseless peasants, this new fear replaced my previous fear of pogrom. What gave it new intensity was the rumor that Elka's two giant sons, Konstantin and Alexander, who grew up with their widowed mother in Krevoya, had joined the bandits. My anxiety increased when I heard Fruma telling my mother that Elka's sons had always been unfriendly to her and at times had accused my aunt of living off the peasants' sweat because she had developed a barter business between the Krevoya peasants' produce and what they needed of Bobruisk's items like clothing, shoes, and inexpensive jewelry. Konstantin, the wilder of the two, bragged that someday he'd take all the rubles she had stashed away.

The expected happened. One evening our door was flung open, and Konstantin's huge frame filled the entrance. The children and I huddled near the brick oven in the center of the room as he removed his rifle from his shoulder and stopped within a few feet of Fruma.

"I want a hundred rubles or I'll kill you." He pointed the rifle at her head.

Sonia, the 12-year-old, let out a wailing cry. I froze with fear.

Fruma took charge.

"Konstantin, you're our neighbor. How could you do this to us?"

"A hundred rubles!"

Sosha, the oldest, spoke up.

"Give it to him, mama."

He followed my aunt to the back of the room, an area partitioned off with a sheet, which was her bedroom. As she was reaching under the cot's bedding, he shouted, "I want it all!" He grabbed the packet that held Fruma's 300 rubles, and with a wave of his gun said, "You're lucky you gave it, or I'd have killed you."

When he left, I tiptoed to the window and saw him head toward the forest, bypassing his mother's house.

The next morning when the peasants heard about the robbery, we were showered with sympathy, except for Elka who remained in her izba and refused to offer an excuse or explanation about what happened. It confirmed the rumor that she had approved of her sons' banditry and used her home to hide their loot.

♣   ♣   ♣   ♣   ♣   ♣

THE COMMUNIST IDEOLOGY that divided families seeped into the parents and children of our two households. I heard Fruma and my mother whispering surreptitiously, something about escaping to America. When I questioned my mother, she gave a vague answer. Was she afraid of me?

One evening, a month after the bandit incident, Fruma and my mother called the children together and Fruma said:

"Your Uncle Itsche is coming early tomorrow morning to take us to Minsk, from where we're going to cross the border to Poland, and then to America. We kept our plans secret because we were afraid some of you might be against it, or one of you might blurt it out to a neighbor, and the neighbor to who knows who else. We're leaving at dawn tomorrow, and none of you are to leave the house until then."

I was thrilled with the idea of going to America, but it also flung up stories I had heard about people who were arrested when it was evident that they were escaping, and also about those who were killed while crossing the border. But I was getting used to living with fear, and the excitement of escape rolled over it.

My heart pounded with adventurous anticipation when I climbed into the wagon for my first step to joining my father in America. Itsche got two horses and a large wagon with room enough to hold our two families and our possessions. We drove through the forested road to Bobruisk, past the beer-smelling area along the Berezina River, along the stench-infested dump that held the city's refuse from the town's outhouses, past Bobruisk's famous fortification walls that held off Napoleon, and finally onto the cobblestone main road that led to Minsk.

We were told by our mothers that it would be a three-day trip and that we'd have to sleep in the wagon at night. The first day was uneventful as the road meandered through sparsely in-habited meadows and thick forest. Sleeping in the wagon was an ordeal, because it was mid-March and the cold penetrated our clothing to the bones. The second day was marred by the stench of corpses lying on the side of the road every few miles. My imagination soared with fear—was it the work of bandits? Communists?

My imagined fears turned into stark reality when we heard the chugging of an automobile approaching us. As it passed, our horses reared at seeing a roaring monster for the first time. They fell on their sides, tipping the wagon and spilling us and our pos-sessions onto the road. The passengers in the automobile, who-ever they were, waved and shouted but didn't stop. Itsche got to his feet, calmed the horses, and because he was a big strong man like my grandfather (his father), he was able to right the horses, who in turn righted the wagon. Some of us were bruised, but not seriously. After getting our belongings into the wagon, we climbed in and were on our way again, grateful that the automobile passengers hadn't stopped to question us.

When we drove through a stretch of thick woods, my eyes darted in all directions, fearful that bandits might materialize at any moment. Usually our conversations stopped at such times, all of us concentrating on the same fear.

Toward evening we drove off the road into a nearby grove of trees, ate our hardboiled eggs, bread, and cooked chicken, and snuggled into the wagon's hay for another bone-chilling night's sleep.

At sunrise we were on our way again. We saw more corpses, and when we heard a car approaching, my uncle would get down from the wagon and hold the horses' manes until it passed. The cold became so unbearable that toward evening my uncle decided to look for a place to spend the night.

We were passing through a small village and picked a house close to the road. The host couple accepted us warmly when my uncle offered to pay ten rubles for our night's stay. I remember that night well, the joy to thaw out my numbed bones and rest my fears. But I remember more vividly what followed.

The next morning, as we were preparing for the final day of our escape, a truck drove up to our wagon and three soldiers got out and walked into the house.

One of them was Vladimir, the young man from Krevoya who expropriated the peasants' grain and cattle.

"You're all under arrest."

"Why, Vladimir?" Fruma took the lead because she knew him since childhood.

"Because you're escaping Russia."

"But we're only going to visit relatives in Minsk," she lied.

"I don't believe you. Search them for money," he ordered.

"But you've been my neighbor, my friend," Fruma pleaded.

"You're not my friend. You're an enemy of Communism!"

They searched my uncle, my mother, Fruma, and were about to search the children. (I had my mother's money sewn in my underwear.) I suddenly grimaced and told our captors that I had to go to the outhouse, and before receiving an answer, I rushed outside to the latrine. (Years later in America, I learned what it meant to be "street smart"; in Russia I had learned how to be "danger smart".) When I got to the outhouse, I quickly ripped off the patch in my underwear, stuffed the rubles in a crack of the floor, covered it with pieces of debris, and walked slowly back to the house.

While they were searching Fruma's children, I was wondering who could have told Vladimir about our leaving Krevoya. Did he have an informer in the village? But that speculative thought didn't last long. When the soldiers found Fruma's rubles on Sosha, and were then finished with searching me, I felt a surge of triumph in outwitting them, followed by the sobering thought of how to retrieve the money that was to pay for crossing the border.

"I'm taking all of you to jail in Minsk," Vladimir announced, "and let them decide what to do with you."

"Can I stay with the couple here?" I asked.

Vladimir didn't seem to mind, and nodded his head.

The first thing I did when they were hauled off to prison was to get the rubles. But that was a slight consolation. In the afternoon I walked the village streets for hours, tears streaming down my cheeks. It was the first time I was ever left alone with strangers, with no way of knowing what was to happen to my mother.

After the bitterest month of my life, a man came one day to take me to Minsk where I found my mother freed, but stricken with pneumonia. Some helpful people put my mother and me in a boxcar that was heading for Bobruisk. My mother was shivering and moaning in my arms. It was bitter cold and we had no food or water. I suppose the jailers freed her because she was near death, and that was the quickest way to get rid of a problem. My uncle and Fruma and her children were released several months later.

As SOON AS RELATIVES nursed my mother back to health, she began planning to escape again. My mother was a tough, resilient woman. With our money intact to spur her on, she persuaded her sister to try again, this time by train.

I remember the stench after we stuffed ourselves into a boxcar packed with people on the night train to Minsk. It was too crowded for police to check the passengers, but when we arrived in Minsk in the morning, several gendarmes scrutinized the crowd before it dispersed in various directions.

I with my bundles and my mother with her two packs walked slowly away from the depot in no particular direction. Fruma and her children separated themselves from us so that we wouldn't attract attention as refugees. My mother and Fruma had never been to Minsk and had no idea what to do next. A half-hour later our families joined again. Our hesitancy attracted the attention of a young girl, and after eyeing us for several minutes, she approached us and said:

"I know what you want."

Afraid she might be an informer, my mother asked timidly:

"How do you know what we want?"

The young girl must have recognized the signs and came directly to the point.

"My father is a smuggler and he'll get you across the border if you have the money."

My mother was a religious person. She concluded that God must have sent her to help us.

"We have the money."

"I have a horse and wagon not far from here. Come with me and I'll drive you to my father."

Her father was a swarthy, big-bellied man who greeted us gruffly and told us we could stay with him until there were signs of a dark night.

In the evening, two days later, he summoned us into his living room and gave instructions how to conduct ourselves during the crossing. We packed ourselves and our possessions into a large wagon, after which he covered us with several layers of hay so that it looked from the outside like any ordinary wagon.

I felt the jarring of the cobblestone city streets for some time and then the smooth surface of a dirt road. I opened a hole in the hay and looked out. Thick, dark forest. When I heard the faint neighing of horses in the distance, the smuggler stopped the wagon and waited. When the neighing stopped, he started again. Several hours later, Fruma's eight-year-old began coughing. The smuggler stopped the wagon, dismounted and pawed through the hay to reach her. Frightened, she began to cry. He slugged her unconscious. Fruma began to weep quietly. The smuggler took the reins again and drove on. The wagon lurched and creaked over bumpy forest terrain for hours while I peered through a hole in the hay watching the dark trunks of trees slowly passing by. Gradually the dark air turned gray, and by the time the sun came up, I felt the wagon rolling downhill. Within minutes, it stopped and the smuggler called out:

"You're in Poland! This is as far as I take you."

I stuck my head out of the hay. We were alongside a cottage. After pawing ourselves out of the wagon and shaking the hay off our clothes, we walked in. A couple greeted us with a calculating look—they were the link in the smuggler's chain to move refugees across the border.

"If you pay them with your possessions," the smuggler told us, "you can stay here a few days until Ivan'll drive you to Horodok, from where you can take a train to Warsaw. I'm going back to Minsk tonight."

As unlucky as we were on our first try to escape, good fortune seemed to follow us this time. My mother lowered her head and offered a few unintelligible words of gratefulness to God, and then lifted her eyes brimming with hope and optimism.

The couple helped themselves to a scarf and a gold watch

from my mother, a gold necklace and earrings from Fruma. The next day the man drove us to Horodok and left us at the home of a Jewish family—another link in the smuggling business.

WE WERE STRANDED in Horodok for six months. Our host family must have been paid by HIAS, an international Jewish agency that helped Jews escape Russia. The family fed, sheltered, and helped us obtain false passports to legitimize our stay in Poland.

Horodok was much bigger than Krevoya and much smaller than Bobruisk—a border town caught in the upheaval of escaping refugees. Those who got into the smuggling business grew rich, but a few paid for it with their lives. Among the many stories that filtered down to my attentive ears was one about the biggest smuggler in Horodok, who made the tragic mistake of bragging about his wealth. One night bandits robbed him of all the loot he had amassed from refugees and killed the smuggler, his wife, and three of his daughters. I remember this incident vividly because at a social gathering I became infatuated with the smuggler's dark-eyed, beautiful 11-year-old daughter. I remember asking her to dance, how she looked at me, and the euphoria of experiencing my first romantic arousal.

The brutal murders reverberated through Horodok for weeks, and in my mind for months. Except for my romantic encounter, I don't remember anything pleasant about Horodok. In fact, I still have a deviated septum from a blow I received from one of the children of our host family who struck me with a spoon across the nose.

I was happy to leave Horodok as we were boarding the train for Warsaw.

I WAS OVERWHELMED with the sight of Warsaw. To me, the tall buildings, the hurrying people, the wide boulevards, the streetcars were as wondrous as seeing the Himalayas for the first time. With the help of HIAS, our two families were taken to two small apartments in a huge building where 20 years later the Jews made a heroic stand against the Nazis and were decimated to the last victim. We lived in this building while waiting for a visa from America.

One day a young man hurried into our apartment and told us to be ready to leave for Valomin within a few hours.

"We've learned there's going to be a sweep of refugee arrests in this building. Get to the railroad station as soon as you can."

While waiting for the train to Valomin with Fruma, her children, and a few other refugee families, I experienced a fright that sticks in my mind to this day. All the passengers at the depot had passed through the boarding gate, but for some reason the inspector checking my mother's passport told her to step aside. The train was about to leave, and my imagination immediately conjured up a scene of being sent back to Russia. Was this to be the end of all our trials?

It seemed from nowhere a man slid up to my mother's side: "Give him twenty zlotes and he'll let you go."

Hesitatingly my mother walked up to the inspector and handed him the money, not knowing what to expect. He took it and waved her to the train. A stranger' small deed, but what a great help to a helpless family wandering across the face of Europe!

Valomin was a quiet little town surrounded by small lakes and forest. It would have been a respite from our wanderings were it not for two new fears. The commandant of the town knew we were there with fake passports, and a representative of HIAS had to bribe him periodically to leave us alone. The other fear was of the children who lived next door. As soon as any of us went out of the house, we were beaten up. The new pogromniks, as we called them, made our lives miserable.

Tired of being cooped up, I generated enough courage one day to leave the house for a nearby lake in the forest. I was transfixed when I got there by a life-and-death scene between a wounded duck and a hunter. I watched from the edge of the lake as the hunter would take a shot at the bird just as it dove under the surface of the water. When it came up many yards away, he would shoot again, but always a second too late. As this went on for about twenty minutes, I began to side with the bird and, looking back, it may have been my first inclination to favor the underdog. The hunter finally gave up, and I got home safely. A small incident, but it lodged in my memory for a long time.

Interspersed with the anguishes of living in Valomin were some pleasant moments. I enjoyed for the first time the delightful taste of ice cream and the miracle of seeing real human figures moving on a screen—the wonder of cinema.

While waiting for the visa, our lifeline to America, my mind kept flinging up images of my father. What did he look like and how would I react to seeing him for the first time? And what would it feel like living without fear?

One day a representative of HIAS walked into the house and, holding up an envelope in his hand, announced:

"I have your visas to America!"

I experienced the greatest joy of my life. My mother enveloped me in her arms. We hugged and kissed and cried.

⊠   ⊠   ⊠   ⊠   ⊠   ⊠

AFTER A TRAIN RIDE from Warsaw to Danzig, we were led to a barracks where we were deloused before boarding a ship to take us across the North Sea to Liverpool, England. The delousing experience was scary. I was led with a hundred naked men and boys into a chalk-white room dotted with black extension heads hanging from the ceiling. Suddenly we were drenched with high velocity hot water. Awkwardly at first, then doing the obvious, we began washing ourselves. It was my first encounter with a shower bath, a lot different than washing myself in Bobruisk and Krevoya in a barrel of rain-water.

The vast volume of water of the North Sea was an unforget-table sight. I had never seen sky and water meet. What becomes mundane by repetition is explosive when seen for the first time. My psyche now changed from fears to wonders. I wallowed in new sights, and they dizzied me.

I wasn't bothered when we were herded in steerage on our way to Liverpool, because it was a new experience. During the three-day crossing, I climbed to one of the higher forbidden decks and watched the waves raise the ship higher and higher; then it would plummet into a trough, and my heart with it.

The steerage stench nauseated me and flattened my mother with seasickness for the entire voyage. But I was mobile and felt a tinge of pride because my mother needed me more than I needed her. I was her only means of getting medicine and what little food she could eat.

Liverpool introduced me to a new wonder: people talking in a strange language—English. The babble of foreign-sounding voices intimidated me. Will I have to learn to speak like that? I tucked the anxiety away and exhilarated in boarding a bigger ship that would finally take us to America.

THE SHIP WE BOARDED at Liverpool to take us to America was huge, and the steerage in which we were packed reeked with suffocating air from the stench of filthy latrines. Within a day out at sea, most of the passengers became so seasick that they were unable to clean up their own vomit. The babble from different languages of strange-looking people turned the bottom of the ship into a stinking menagerie. Mingling with this stench was the nauseating smell of greasy food that retched up more heaving misery.

My mother was a physically strong woman, but her seasickness drained her into a helpless invalid. In between her moanings that she'd rather die than continue with her suffering, I brought her food, water, medicine, and—one time when she passed out—a doctor. When she was revived, I heard her murmur, "If I knew it would be so bad, I'd never have left Bobruisk!"

With wobbly legs, churning stomach, and swimming head, I tended to her needs, occasionally leaving for a few gulps of fresh air on one of the upper decks.

After seventeen grueling days, my mother had to be carried off the ship on a stretcher when we landed in Newfoundland. From there we took a train to New York, and then another to Milwaukee.

Seeing my moustached, five-foot, rotund father (half a head shorter than my mother) was less than an enthusiastic experience. We embraced, but I felt I was holding onto a stranger. I tried but couldn't generate a gushing emotion, in contrast to my mother, who, though emaciated, hugged him amorously.

We boarded a streetcar at the Milwaukee depot, and arrived at my father's flat over a butcher shop on Seventh and Lloyd streets. After a relaxing sleep in a comfortable bed, I got up the next morning to face the challenge of a new life in America.

2

AN ILLITERATE IN A STRANGE LAND

*I Was a Plodding Turtle among
Prancing Rabbits.*

MICHELANGELO MUST HAVE HAD MORE CONfidence carving the statue of David from a slab of marble than I had carving a small niche in America. Street signs and store signs were as strange to me as hearing people talk in unintelligible sounds. What would learning be like? I had never gone to school or had to learn anything.

I faced a new kind of apprehension when I walked into what was called the "greenhorn" school. Males and females from 10 to 60 years, from Germany, Czechoslovakia, Russia, Norway, etc., were sitting around long bare tables, talking in their different languages.

A husky, no-nonsense-looking woman teacher announced in a clear loud voice: "We're all going to learn how to speak English, and I'm going to teach you."

Of course, we didn't know what she said, until a bilingual representative of each country explained it to us.

We nodded our heads and waited. The teacher put her hand over her mouth to indicate that we should stop talking. However, a Russian woman of about twenty, who I remembered crossed the Atlantic with us, kept on jabbering to her neighbor.

Our teacher, with ruler in hand, tapped her on the head. To the surprise of the ''greenhorns'' and the teacher, the Russian got up from her table and hit the teacher full in the face. There was an instantaneous uproar of laughter and babble in many languages. The teacher, apparently used to such surprises, nonchalantly called a guard from an adjoining room who led the girl out of the class.

Several teachers with the help of part-time interpreters taught us enough rudimentary English so that most of the older pupils were satisfied and dropped out, while the young stayed on and advanced at a faster pace.

After six months of intense listening and diligent study, I was chosen to recite the Pledge of Allegiance at what was designated to be a graduation from the ''greenhorn'' school to regular American classes. At thirteen, my head was spinning with trepidation at the prospect of doing what any American kindergarten child could have done better than I.

After graduation, I was thrust into the sixth grade with American students who were two to three years younger than I. With my heavy Yiddish accent, I was as much an oddity to them as they were a source of wonder to me. They were much smarter than I, more carefree, and full of fun. None of them took books home, while I lugged them for homework every day. I was a plodding turtle among prancing rabbits.

Among the brightest in the class were Joe Goisman and Herman Hurwitz. Joe eventually became an orthopedic surgeon and Herman an attorney. Because I was different and looked up to them, they took a shine to me and decided to help Americanize me. I had difficulty with V's and W's, saying ''wery vell'' for ''very well''. They made a deal with me that every time they heard me use *V* for *W* or *W* for *V*, I had to pay each a nickel. I made an extra effort to speak slowly and correctly in their presence until eventually I licked the problem. In other ways, such as introducing me to American sports and slang, they gradually converted me to the rhythm of American life.

My graduating into high school was like a hillbilly graduating into Harvard. I could handle the freshmen—I was older and had gotten used to them in grade school—but the upperclassmen, especially the seniors, were beyond my reach in sophistication and learning. How could they participate in outside activities like plays, football, cheerleading and other extracurricular activities and still keep up with their schoolwork? I wondered. I labored while most of them playfully breezed through their subjects. Was I a slow learner? Did the hardships of my past have anything to do with it? I was disturbed at my inability to think as fast as my friends. I compensated by putting out an extraordinary effort to keep up with them. The minus became a plus. I was prepared to get some splinters in my hands while climbing the ladder to keep up with my peers. That attitude set me on a basic course to overcoming obstacles.

Hard work didn't burden me. On the contrary, I became happier, livelier, more American. My foreign accent became less noticable. I swept myself into my peer mannerisms with enthusiasm. Fruma's children and others who clung to their Russian ways retained their accents and never fully integrated into the American culture.

A new world opened up when I became literate. The meaning of words, the ideas they jointly conveyed, made my imagination soar. Novels fascinated me, especially Jack London's *The Call of the Wild*. His descriptions of rugged men and fierce dogs enchanted me. And *Martin Eden*, by the same author, introduced me to the romantic fragrance of a tender love story. His realism sent my own romantic juices flowing.

I fell in love with books. After reading them, I'd write book reports—not for school, but for my own edification. This interest opened a "dialogue" between me and authors that's lasted to this day.

I BEGAN MY COLLEGE freshman year as a completely homogenized American. I lost my accent and wholeheartedly embraced my peers' cultural traits. None could tell that I had been born in Russia. But more than my success in becoming Americanized, I wanted to become a scholar, a goal that eluded me. One of my professors summed up my failure with: "You talk like an *A*, but you write exams like a *C*." With my limited ability, I reconciled myself to the reality that striving and failing to do the impossible still leaves room for the possible, and that wasn't so bad. It satisfied me.

While most of my student friends were singling out courses for a specific lifework—law, medicine, business, or teaching—I chose general courses to prepare myself for becoming a novelist.

I had read that people are generally divided into right-brainers and left-brainers. The left-brainers had a knack for detail, like accounting, medicine, law, etc., and right-brainers were generalists and conceptualists. To salve my inability to get *A*'s that required detail, I persuaded myself that I was a right-brainer. My college friends weren't sympathetic to my theory. They preferred to dub me as a dreaming dilettante.

"You're in the clouds," they chided. "You'll have to come down to earth where the action is, if you want to get along in the real world."

My two closest friends got into the "real world" when they were juniors. They bought football tickets from students for a dollar apiece and scalped them at the game for three to ten dollars. They made a bundle. I was envious. To show them that I too was in the "real world," I bought a friend's ticket for a seat that happened to be next to mine and hurried out to the game to sell it. Many people were milling around at the gate. I picked a likely football fan and approached him.

"Want a couple of tickets on the thirty-yard line?"

"Yes . . . and you're under arrest for scalping!"

My legs wobbled. Blood drained from my face. Would I be expelled like others for scalping?

"Sir," I said trembling, "would you believe that this is the first time I ever tried this? All I have is my friend's ticket and mine, that's all." And I showed them to him.

He looked at me for a few seconds and must have recognized that I was a small fish in this business.

"I believe you. Will you promise not to ever try this again?"

I was overwhelmed with gratitude.

"I not only promise. Here, take the tickets as my punishment."

He smiled and walked away. I headed for my room with a mixture of confusing thoughts.

The next day when I told my two experienced scalping friends what had happened, they diminished me with their laughter.

"You're just not cut out for business, George. Stick to your heavenly philosophy and leave the earthly action to us."

Several weeks later my two friends were caught with their extensive scalping operation and put on probation. It strengthened by conviction that it's safer in the ivory tower than in the practical machinations below.

☑   ☑   ☑   ☑   ☑   ☑

My interest in idealism turned me toward introversion, away from the street-savvy extroversion. However, my idealism didn't rush me into a crusading zeal. It led me to a balanced rationality. I had a chance to test this attitude in a unique incident.

A group of communist students held a protest rally for some cause on the shore of Lake Mendota. Several members of the University of Wisconsin football team stormed the meeting and, in a spirit of fun, dumped some of the leaders into the lake. The spectators howled with laughter. I didn't. It reminded me of the pogrom hooligans who also did it for fun, but more violently.

The next day, *The Daily Cardinal* student newspaper charged editorially:

"Student fascists use brute force to counter ideas. They deserve expulsion."

The conservative students countered:

"We applaud the dunking. It's about time someone cooled off these crazy commies."

My approach to the incident was evenhanded. While I didn't condone it, neither did I have any sympathy for the communists' intensity, sloppy clothes, and arrogance. They acted like they were above the herd intellectually, as the WASPS did socially.

≋   ≋   ≋   ≋   ≋   ≋

IN PREPARATION FOR my writing career, I would occasionally do a human-interest feature and have it published in the *Milwaukee Journal*. While looking for such a story, I found a black student who was working his way through school. We had eyed each other several times as strangers, and then one day I asked him if we could talk awhile. He invited me to his one-room basement apartment in one of the university buildings.

"What's it like to be the only black among 15,000 students, and how do you feel about us?"

He smiled and I could tell he had matured beyond his age.

"It's a privilege, and I've no negative or positive feelings about the students. They ignore me, and I ignore them. If someone shows an interest, I return it."

"I'm interested. Care to reveal your feelings?"

"The pioneers always lead a more interesting life. *I'm a pioneer.* I'm grateful for the challenge to be here. What I learn I'll pass on to my brothers and sisters. I have a greater responsibility than the average student here. *You* have an education to get; *I* have *that*, and *more*—to further the welfare of my people."

My intention to spend an hour stretched into three. We became good friends.

⚱   ⚱   ⚱   ⚱   ⚱   ⚱

IN CONTRAST TO the serious episode with the thoughtful black student, I fell prey to an embarrassing incident that dogged me until my graduation.

At a formal senior student party, my date and I, and two other couples, decided to take a boat ride in separate rowboats on Lake Mendota before getting into the festivities. As we were returning from our twilight ride, my date stood up prematurely and, losing her footing, fell into the water. I didn't know how to swim, but I jumped in after her, probably relying on my two nearby friends to save both of us. To my joyful surprise the water was only four feet deep. I put my arm around my girlfriend and walked the twenty feet to shore.

But my joy was short-lived. The two couples couldn't stop laughing. We must have looked ridiculous in our drenched formal clothes.

"Please, Joe," I said to one of my friends who was a known prankster, "don't run with this to the *Cardinal*."

"Would I do that to you?"

He did. The next afternoon someone hailed me from a half block away.

"My hero!"

In my sociology class some of the students looked at me and snickered. After class I ran to get the *Cardinal*. I blanched at the lead story:

"STUDENT HERO JUMPS INTO FOUR FEET OF WATER TO SAVE HIS GIRLFRIEND."

I provided entertainment for students for weeks. They razzed, while I squirmed.

≈   ≈   ≈   ≈   ≈   ≈

MY INTROVERTED INTEREST in books and my idealism put a dent in my social life. The majority of college girls seemed interested only in what they called the fun-lane—lively talk, drinking, and especially someone who owned a car. Because I didn't qualify in any of these ways, they didn't seek me out; and because they weren't my kind, neither did I pursue them.

I was looking for what I was reading in romantic novels—flirtation, infatuation, courtship—in waltz-time progression. But this was the flapper age, and I didn't fit. However, I didn't mind being on the outside, because I was convinced I was on the right side.

Sometimes the lines between their side and my side blurred. When I was a senior, a junior student encouraged a flirtation that stirred my romantic juices. I suggested a walk in the woods off campus, and she agreed. We enjoyed talking about each other's interests. The second date developed into infatuation and the beginning of courtship. On the third date, she casually suggested that we rent a room in a hotel for a weekend. I stumbled for an answer. I didn't want my romantic progression to end so soon, and besides, I was thinking of a friend who was suffering from a strong dose of syphilis. When she saw hesitancy instead of enthusiasm, she dropped the suggestion—and with it our relationship. We were out of step: I was waltzing, she was fox-trotting.

I HAD MADE MANY CHANGES in my life, but a few remained. I had been eating kosher food through high school and my first two years in college. Because of my kosher conditioning, I did not eat in restaurants. However, peer pressure finally prevailed. Eating in a restaurant for the first time and tasting ham a few months later were two emotional experiences—prosaic to my friends, but adventurous for me.

My religious orthodoxy took a jolt when I quit eating kosher food. As I delved in my philosophical and sociological readings, I reduced what little Jewish rite and rote I followed to indifference. I was neither an atheist nor an observing Jew. When I went home for the high holy days, it was out of respect for my parents rather than out of any feeling for God. Most of my Jewish friends were adrift in the same grey zone. Our focus was on our careers, not on finding something big to live for.

When I was handed my diploma with which to face the world, I had no abiding purpose or noble cause, nor was I trained for anything. My only plan for the future was to become a novelist.

3

SHATTERED DREAMS—NEW HORIZONS

*I Was Desperate—Not Robust Enough for
Blue-Collar Labor, Nor Trained for
White-Collar Work.*

WITHIN DAYS AFTER GRADUATION, I POUNCED upon my writing career. My mother tidied up a room for me and told friends and relatives that her son had begun working on a great Russian novel. She really wanted me to be a lawyer or doctor; but not to hurt my feelings, she supported my choice. My father was too preoccupied with trying to earn a living in his shoe-repair shop to offer any opinion about my career.

I would spring out of bed every morning and write feverishly all day. The plot of my novel had the backdrop of the Russian Revolution, and much of the material was autobiographical. When words, phrases, and sentences flowed easily, the day would end in a satisfying glow. As weeks turned into months, I became more immersed in my work, and more introvertive. I read less and spent less time with my friends. I became more involved with my fictional characters.

Gradually the inner glow began to fade as I began to realize that my writing was too ordinary to excite a publisher. Combining suspense, logical sequences, and vivid characters was a lot more difficult than I thought. Experienced writers who read my manuscript didn't spare my feelings. "Not good enough," was the general consensus. And I believed them. I had read enough good literature to know that my writing paled by comparison.

After having built up the steam of enthusiasm, the letdown was unbearably deflating and I became listless, discouraged. A gray, hopeless mood set in. I walked the streets with glazed eyes, my mind in turmoil. Thoughts chased one another in utter confusion. I didn't have the resources to quiet my mind, to dissipate the psychic trauma.

In desperation, I turned to Harold, a fellow graduate who, like me, was writing unpublishable stuff: poetry. To support himself, he huckstered watermelons from a horse and wagon during the summer. In the winter, he hibernated to write his poetry. I was looking at an unkempt, slovenly man who turned his back on society and lived solely within his poetic universe. We had a long discussion about our careers, and it clarified my thinking. I didn't like what I saw in Harold—an unbalanced life. It suited him, but not me. I decided to give up writing and look for something else.

But what? I was not robust enough for blue-collar labor, nor trained for white-collar work. Since I had some experience in writing, I applied for a job with the *Milwaukee Journal*. The interviewer smiled at my eagerness. Experienced writers who had worked for the paper for years had been let go to cut expenses.

I applied to a half dozen advertising agencies and got the same negative reply. I took several examinations for government agency jobs. I wasn't called. My professor's analysis rang in my ears—"You talk like an *A*, but write exams like a *C*."

I was enduring the opposite of what I had experienced during my novel-writing days. Then I would jump out of bed full of enthusiasm and hope. Now, when I opened my eyes, I would stare at the ceiling and forlornly face another empty day.

SO DESPERATE HAD I BECOME, that when I read a book about the adventures of hoboing in America, I decided to try it just to get out of my unbearable rut and perhaps earn some money writing about it. As much as I tried to remain rational during those doleful days, the hoboing idea slid me off into the irrational.

The first day, I hitchhiked about a hundred miles from home and got permission from a farmer to sleep in his hayloft. In the morning, after shaking the hay off my clothes and sneezing the dust out of my nose, I was attacked by the farmer's dog. Fortunately, he shooed him away before I was bitten. I thanked him and hit the road again. After three days, my wanderlust waned, and dejectedly I hitchhiked back to face my empty hours.

How I envied the plumbers, electricians, and carpenters! They could plan their lives around their work. When I was in college and dealt with worldly affairs, I didn't think I would ever envy the life of a craftsperson. I did now. I even took a positive look at my father's work. He was a master at making new shoes and repairing old ones. He was happily making a living, while I was getting nowhere with my college knowledge.

At 26, while my mind was grinding frustratingly with no grist to grind, it would turn occasionally to my urges for marital mating. I wanted a wife and children to round out my life. I wasn't exactly a "catch," but because I talked like an *A*, a few young women showed some interest in me. As our common interests grew, I would nevertheless—and reluctantly—cut off these relationships, because I had nothing to offer except interesting conversation. This added another dimension to my helplessness. How long would this situation last? The psychic trauma was more pervasive than physical fear. In Russia, my hope of escape left room for optimistic enthusiasm; but now the mix of adult responsibility and a bleak future replaced the liveliness of hope with deathlike despair.

After two years of groping, grasping, pleading for work, and being rejected, my despondency slid into the deep recesses of my mind. It paralyzed me. I stopped fighting. Some days I walked the streets with aimless indifference. Only the patient understanding and security of my parents kept me from veering off the plane of sanity.

A FRIEND OF MINE offered a glimmer of hope when he suggested that I publish a magazine about the beverage industry, now that Prohibition was over and the manufacture of beer and liquor was legalized. It sounded logical and I grasped at it. The writing aspect excited me; but how to make it pay? Also, I thought: If I can't get a job, why not create my own? Thoughts, like magnets, often attract other supportive thoughts. While I was checking the cost of printing a thousand copies of a sixteen-page magazine, someone suggested the name of a salesman who had connections with newly forming distilleries, breweries, and taverns. The salesman convinced me that he could sell $1,000 per month of advertising to cover the $500 cost of printing, leaving a $500 profit, if I wrote interesting copy catering to the newly revived beverage industry.

I immediately went to work gathering information about the history of liquor, wine, and beer. I wrote how beverages were first used as a food, then to romanticize celebrations and sacralize ceremonials. I titled the magazine *Beverage Guide*. The general tone of my articles, with appropriate pictures, aimed at uplifting the image of the beverage industry. We got enough advertising to publish four monthly issues. Then the money dried up—or rather found its way into my salesman's pocket.

I hired another salesman, and at the end of four months, as we were beginning to show a slight profit, a new problem arose. I had to attend meetings of the Tavern Keepers Association, where the members would hoist a few too many and talk in a manner I wasn't used to. And what was extremely bothersome was the custom of buying each other drinks. I felt uncomfortable with my obligation to drink with them. My gut feeling was that I wasn't cut out for this work.

Y   Y   Y   Y   Y   Y

As I LOOK BACK, what added to my dislike of the liquor business was the unhappy memory of my father rigging up a small distillery in the attic of our home during Prohibition, where he distilled two or three gallons of whiskey a week and sold them to government officials. He was doing it to augment his meager income from his shoe-repair shop. I was against it for several reasons: It was against the law; I was worried that the attic might catch on fire; and I feared that my father would be arrested and jailed.

I didn't prevail. So I was relieved when Prohibition ended and my father dismantled his miniature distillery.

The combination of the unhappy memory of my father's whiskey venture and what I saw liquor doing to people I dealt with soured my work and put me in a quandary as to what to do next.

My problem was solved when two men with Al Capone hats walked into my $10-a-month office and said:

"We're coming into Wisconsin with a tabloid called *The Tavern*. You're a nice young man and we'll pay you $10 a week to be our editor, but we'll tell you what to write. Your *Beverage Guide* is too fancy. You've got to write what interests the tavern keepers—not about beverage history. If you don't take our offer, we suggest you fold up. There's not enough room for two.

They looked menacing, based on what I'd seen of Mafia pictures and stories I had read about Al Capone.

"Let me think it over," I said, and they left.

There wasn't much to think over. Instead of being sad, I was glad. With a mixture of relief from an unpleasant work environment and a gnawing feeling of facing empty hours again, I quit publishing the *Beverage Guide*.

I WENT BACK to my barren existence. The work I left, though disagreeable, was less sterile than the emptiness of no work.

One day while lying on the sofa gazing at the ceiling, a new thought crossed my mind. What if my friends were wrong that I wasn't cut out to be a businessman? In desperation, and with trepidation, I walked into a two-man real-estate office and asked for a job to sell homes on commission. They had nothing to lose, so they hired me. I was too shy to offer my zero selling abilities to a large professional brokerage firm.

One of the partners dabbled in brokering mortgages, and the other in selling homes. They were two nice, middle-aged men who worked in my favorite tempo—waltz time.

They loaded me with calls to show properties because they preferred to work behind their desks. One of the first calls was to show a home on the south side, about seven miles from our office. I had a poor sense of direction, and still do, so I asked the young couple for the best route to our listing. The man eagerly explained the best way to get there. When we got to the home, I pointed out the special amenities as well as the defects, and how to finance their purchase. I must have sounded sincere, because when I returned to the office, they told my boss they liked the way I handled them and believed what I said. He signed them up.

It was a lucky first sale! I earned $200—twenty times what I got for a feature article that took a week to research and write! I could hardly believe what happened to me. I was ecstatic. "What was it that made the young couple believe me?'' I asked myself. Was it sincerity? Could that be an important selling tool? I gave it a lot of thought. As I kept showing houses, I found myself genuinely liking the young couples who were looking to make the biggest purchases of their lives. Milwaukee has many ethnic groups and out of their diversified cultures I learned a common-denominator truth: Beyond their conditioned ethnicity, they all had a responsive goodness when they saw and believed that someone was trying to help them. That truth made an indelible mark on my mind.

Because I honored and nurtured that truth, they invited me to their homes, offered me their food, and philosophized about their religions and cultures. Caring for their real-estate needs was practical, educational, and joyful. I began receiving referrrals from their friends and relatives. I was inundated with calls, and my business adrenalin roared with enthusiasm.

But my success created a problem with the two partners. Since the custom in the real-estate business was for salesmen to receive half of the sales commission, and since they gave me most of the calls, I was earning more than each of my bosses! To remedy the inequity, they cut my commission to one-third. Because I was doing so fabulously well, I didn't object.

In 1937, I earned $6,000—a sum beyond my wildest expectations. My marital urgings came back with full force. I zeroed in on a beautiful young maiden, and this time, instead of backing away when it got serious, I proposed. But it was almost too late. An attorney was putting up serious competition. For half a year it was touch and go between us. Had I not had the $6,000 in the bank, I would have backed off. But backed by it, and by my new-found sales ability, I confidently courted with the finesse of an *A*, and won.

And what a wonderful victory as I look back on 55 years of marital harmony!

THE MOMENTUM of my success propelled me into making a risky business decision: to start my own company. In my mental battle between confidence and caution, confidence won. I rented a one-room office and began advertising for listings.

Milwaukee was, and still is, a conservative city. The habits of its many ethnic groups changed slowly. The large, well-known professional real-estate offices had, in those days, institutionalized the custom of listing properties for six months and advertising them infrequently to save expenses. I had to come up with an unusual idea to compete against them.

Why not advertise that I can sell a home in 30 days? I inserted an ad that read:

IF YOUR PRICE IS RIGHT

I CAN SELL YOUR HOME

IN 30 DAYS!

I began getting calls from prospects, but also from the Board of Realtors, of which I was a member. I was asked to appear before the Executive Committee to explain why I was rocking the rock-ribbed rule of listing properties for six months. I defended my 30-day idea with the argument that by concentrating the advertising in a shorter period, homes would sell faster, and also, it wasn't fair to keep an anxious seller dangling for six months. My arguments must have prevailed, because the Board didn't press their complaint.

When I sold several of my listings within the 30 days, I took the idea a step further. I ran an ad with the following copy:

HERE'S THE PROOF

WHY WE CAN SELL YOUR

PROPERTY IN 30 DAYS

1. 1230 Columbia Street
   SOLD IN 18 DAYS

2. 1840 N. 35th Street
   SOLD IN 12 DAYS

3. 5360 N. 18th Street
   SOLD IN 5 DAYS

Within one year, I became one of Milwaukee's leading brokers in home sales. I was amazed that such a simple idea could do so much. I had to hire several salesmen to handle the increased business.

  ☏ ☏ ☏ ☏ ☏ ☏

MY BURST OF SUCCESS got me to thinking. Was I proving that I was an *A* in conceiving? That conceptualizing was my strength?

One day I tried an experiment. I sat down, stilled my mind, and waited for some new concept to strike. It was my first attempt at meditation (about which, more later).

It worked! One of the listings in my office was a property with six cottages on one lot. It was a run-down investment piece that successive owners kept milking, with little effort at rejuvenating it. Instead of trying to sell it, I bought if for $6,000—the listed price. I decided to try something that had never been done before in Milwaukee—divide it into six parcels and sell them to six different owners. After painting the exteriors and landscaping the area, I sold each for $1,500—

several of them to the tenants. The new handymen owners remodeled the neglected cottages into attractive, liveable homes. Everyone came out ahead: the idea created six proud homeowners, a piece of city blight was turned into an oasis of pleasant living-space, and I earned $3,000.

But my innovative idea raised the dander of the *Milwaukee Journal*'s real-estate editor:

"Bockl hasn't provided clear title to the owners of the cottages," he accused. "They have to share common walkways, the same water system, and the same garbage area. He's created a legal jungle."

Little did he and I know that 20 years later, people owning condominiums would even share the hallways of a condominiumized apartment building. Neither of us knew that I had stumbled onto the embryonic stage of the condominium concept.

It was an original idea that earned hundreds of thousands of dollars in commissions for my salesmen and my fledgling company. We subdivided dozens of neglected multi-parceled properties into individually owned homes and upgraded many parts of the city.

Encouraged by my success, I took the idea a step further. A speculator built twelve 8-family units on ten acres on the outskirts of town and couldn't sell them because there were few investors for a large project. I took a quiet, meditative walk, stilled my mind, and waited for some insight to strike. It did. Why not handle the twelve 8-family project the way I did the six-cottage deal? The logic followed the insight. There are more 8-family buyers than 96-unit apartment buyers. There are fewer investors willing to take the greater risk.

Managing risk is crucial in the real estate business. During several quiet times, I developed a rudimentary concept to handle risk taking. It consisted of four prerequisites: guts, imagination, persuasion, and integrity. I likened it to a four-legged table. If any one of the four legs is missing, the table will wobble. Without guts, a project is stillborn; without imagination, limitation sets in; without persuasion, nothing happens; and without integrity, it's difficult to obtain financing.

I felt I had the last three. All I needed was guts. I bought the project for $350,000 and within six months I sold each 8-family for $40,000 and realized a profit of $130,000. Dividing the whole into twelve legally separate parcels proved more difficult than the sales, because the lawyers were still new at condominiumizing.

ɾ   ɾ   ɾ   ɾ   ɾ   ɾ

IN ONE OF MY meditative moments, a strange thought crossed my mind. I was wonderfully led. By whom? By God? The question remained unanswered as a feeling of gratefulness swept over me, followed by a suffusion of thankfulness to the many people who had turned me down for jobs. Had they hired me, I could have remained on a salary that paid one-tenth of what I was earning now. All of my former minuses turned to plusses. Something led me from a potential lifelong cul-de-sac to an open highway of opportunity.

By many standards I was ordinary, especially in handling detail, and would have remained a colorless mediocrity had I not gained confidence in my conceptual ability and ridden it from where I was to unexpected progress. Of course, I was a mere popgun in business, but within my ordinary capacities, I was an extraordinary success.

I began to view problems as challenges. When one is in that mindset, opportunities arise in many forms. One of my vexing problems involved selling homes to Afro-Americans in white neighborhoods. Most real-estate brokers stayed away from such sales because of white owners' resistance and the difficulties of mortgaging Afro-American home purchases.

In the early 1950s, prejudice was rife and desegregation was new. Should I get involved with white prejudice and black buyers who are not mortgageable? I asked myself during one of my quiet times. Should I help the blacks at the expense of the whites?

I chose the underdog.

I assigned part of my salesforce to sell adjoining white-owned houses to black buyers. I was called a blockbuster. I cushioned the false accusations with the good feeling that I was helping blacks to break out of their congested ghetto.

Financing black home sales was as acute a problem as prejudice. Many Savings and Loan Associations, in effect, redlined neighborhoods when they demanded large down payments and excellent credit ratings before making loans to blacks. There were many willing black buyers and as many reluctant white lenders.

How to break the impasse?

The answer came one morning—an answer that satisfied the seller, buyer, lender, and my organization. Here's how it worked:

The Bockl Company would buy a $10,000 home or duplex from a white seller, sign an $8,500 mortgage to a Savings and Loan, and add my $1,500 to pay off the seller in cash.

We would then sell the property to a black family for $12,000, with $500 down, and take a second mortgage of $3,000—the difference between the $8,500 first mortgage we owed and the $11,500 balance the buyer owed us.

In order to get back the $1,500 we put into the deal plus a brokerage commission, we sold the $3,000 second mortgage at a discount for $2,000, and with the $500 we got in cash from the buyer, we got our $1,500 plus a brokerage fee of $1,000.

With this type of financing, where I became personally liable for millions of dollars in loans, we were able to sell 600 homes to black families who could not otherwise have become homeowners. We stretched out the second mortgage payments over the same 25-year amortization period as the first mortgage, so that the buyer's total payment was little more than rent.

Our plan converted renters into homeowners—a societal

stabilizer. As we expected, it didn't work perfectly. Many of these new owners left town or moved out without notice, leaving us to make the first mortgage payments and, in many cases, wiping out the second-mortgage equities. But approximately 550 of the 600 new homeowners not only made their payments, but increased their equities and traded their properties for higher-priced ones as they moved further out into white neighborhoods.

The plan had many beneficial rippling effects. It created new homeowners, originated safe mortgages for the Savings and Loan industry (they were guaranteed by me personally), sold homes of white owners who wished to move further out, and provided jobs for my salespeople.

Even as I was receiving the slings and arrows from my accusers, I knew that what I was doing was good for the blacks who were eager to become homeowners, for the whites who wanted to sell their homes to move elsewhere, for the city, for desegregation, and for the Bockl Real Estate Company. It was a five Win-Win-Win-Win-Win venture that benefited all participants.

5   5   5   5   5   5   5

MY BUSINESS WAS MUSHROOMING and I needed more salespersons. I decided to handpick them rather than rely on the Help Wanted columns. But how? The answer came when I was watching an amateur play one evening at a social center, where I was particularly impressed with one of the actors. At the end of the play, I walked up to him.

"What do you do for a living?"

Sheepishly he replied:

"I'm a garbage inspector. I work for the city."

I had him in my office the next morning, and after an hour's discussion, Ted Marks joined my firm. He was associated with me for twenty years, then formed his own company, and is now retired in a $300,000 home—living in semi-luxury, and doing pro-bono work in his community.

While doing some work in my study one day, I heard a salesman with a German accent trying to sell a carpet-cleaner to my wife. He was doing a superb selling job. I walked out of my room and got him into conversation.

"Are you satisfied with your job?"

"Not really."

I had him in my office the next morning, and Gus Wand joined my organization. He became one of my top salesmen for ten years, after which he formed his own home-building company and became a millionaire.

My tennis buddy was a schoolteacher. He moved slowly but methodically, both on the tennis court and in decision-making.

"Others joined your company," he explained logically, "because they had poor jobs, and had nothing much to lose. But I've got a good teaching position with many fringe benefits. Not easy to give it up."

"But those who gave up their poor jobs," I said, "are earning twice as much as you with your good job."

After six months of hesitancy, Ralph Schwartz gave up teaching and joined my organization. He was associated with me for twenty years, earning five times what he had been earning as a teacher.

Even my two university friends, Joe Goodman and Joe Waxer, who had convinced me in college that I was not cut out to be a businessman, gave up their jobs and joined my firm.

Others whose talents at school far outshone mine used my company as a stepping-stone for their future careers. In the process, they poured their prodigious abilities into my organization, building it into the fastest-growing in the city.

Joe Zilber, an attorney, worked for me for three years and then developed one of the largest building companies in the nation. He's reputed to be worth over $200 million.

Larry Katz, who was associated with me for four years, became the Federal Housing Administrator for the State of Wisconsin.

Horace Rosen, whose salesmanship could charm the gold out of a buyer's teeth, made a tremendous contribution during his five years with me, then formed his own company and became a millionaire.

There was an abundance of raw talent available at the time, and I was fortunate to have the available vehicle for these people to get started. By the early 1950s, I had 45 salespersons with some of the best brains in the city—graduate engineers, economists, lawyers, social workers, English majors—many of whom had graduated at the top of their classes.

When the business activity became too much for me to handle, I hired Paul Spector, a managerial genius with an elephantine memory. With his fatherly touch and orderly mind, he did a far better job of managing the sales staff than I.

It wasn't my training that prepared my staff to form their own businesses, it was their high-caliber abilities. I knew which ones would leave me; but I hired them anyway, because I reasoned: Why not utilize their sales genius for as long as I could keep them?

At first, I was bothered when they set up competitive offices; but when I took the annoyance to my quiet time and evaluated it, I was able to dissolve it. Hadn't I done the same thing myself? When sales stars like Joe Zilber, Horace Rosen, Gus Wand, and others left, I thanked them for their contributions and wished them success.

Because as many as 25 new firms grew out of my office, my organization came to be known as The Bockl College of Real Estate Knowledge. I liked it, especially when I thrived in the midst of my own created competition.

My earnings from the real-estate brokerage business were modest, even though we were closing a sale a day. Large advertising costs, generous profit sharing, and managerial overhead left me with an average of $75,000 a year. It was certainly adequate, but my sights were on new challenges with greater risks.

4

HOW PIONEERING BUILT A LOCAL REAL ESTATE EMPIRE

*I Was Attracted to Pioneering—I Wanted to
Be a Locomotive Instead of a Caboose.*

A MIRACLE, IN THE ULTIMATE SENSE OF THE WORD, requires supernatural intervention. A near-miracle is within human capacity, but it requires superhuman effort mixed with a great deal of luck.

Flushed with my brokerage success, I began thinking about doing a real-estate venture on a grand scale—preferably something that had never been done before. As the Bible says, "Seek, and ye shall find." I found it; but it took a near-miracle to mold all the uncertainties into certainty.

In 1954, I attended a Building Owners and Managers Association Convention in Denver. One of the attractions was a tour of that city's newest modern office building.

After listening to several lectures on the intricacies of building, leasing, and financing new office buildings, I began toying with the idea of building the first modern, centrally air-conditioned office building in my city.

At first, my human logic dismissed this as a whimsical idea. My real-estate experience had been limited to selling homes. But the challenge persisted with these disturbing thoughts: Was a new office building needed? Could I finance it? Could I lease it? Where should I build it?

Back of these thoughts welled up a wave of confidence. It pushed my imagination to play with the uncertainties until I reached the conviction that they were not beyond solution, provided I faced the obstacles with more than ordinary effort.

Convinced that a new office building was needed, and that I could fill that need, I bought a two-acre parcel of land for $200,000 two miles from downtown and spent $25,000 in architectural fees with a 30-year-old architect who shared my enthusiasm to do the unusual.

With two obstacles out of the way, I now faced the third hurdle—obtaining a $3 million mortgage. I was turned down with "What chutzpah!" looks by a half-dozen banks and insurance companies.

What do I do now? I wondered. Why not try a local Savings and Loan Association—my last resort.

I chose the largest, The Mutual Savings and Loan, and presented my reasons for the viability of a new office building to its 85-year-old president.

"The largest loan we've ever made," he said after a week of trying to get an appointment with him, "was $300,000. Tell me, young man: why should we risk $3 million on an unconventional loan to an untried developer?"

The question triggered all my arguments. With six months of practice, I recited them fluently and then added, "Why don't you meet my boldness with yours: I build the first modern office building, and you make the first unconventional loan."

"I like your spunk," he smiled. "Let me think about it."

He was a gutsy, self-made man who must have wanted this audacious loan to be one of his last hurrahs, to show his competitors that he still had a lot of dare left. Also, he was a very shrewd lender. He knew that our city was ripe for a new office building.

However, to protect his association and his reputation, he limited his risk by requiring that I put up all I owned as collateral—$300,000 worth of properties and my $200,000 free-

and-clear lot. He wrote a clause into the mortgage that if I failed to lease 50 percent of the space within eight months, I would forfeit my $500,000, and the association would complete the building and become its owner.

When the loan was consummated, the consensus of the rumor-mongers was that I was foolish to risk my entire fortune for a pipe dream—and that the aging president of the association approved the loan out of senility. I now faced my fourth and last obstacle—leasing 200,000 square feet of office space. After three months of hard work, I had stirred up a lot of interest—but only 10 percent of signed leases.

I had drawn floor plans for 10,000 square feet for General Motors, 7000 for Prudential Life Insurance, 5000 for Mutual of New York, 4000 for Zurich of Switzerland, and others, but they all hesitated, each waiting for the others to sign first. They were skeptical of my ability to complete the building in time, if at all, and guarantee their moving-in dates. The crisis became a log jam of indecision, and my time was running out.

Then a flicker of hope!

The Milwaukee General Motors manager was a kindly man who liked my plans (the unlimited parking didn't hurt, either) but refused to sign because "I can't take the risk of entering into a lease and not being sure of moving in. If you can get my superior to say yes, I'll say yes too."

"Where's your superior?"

"In New York."

"Will you call him for me?"

"No—I'd rather you did it yourself."

Within a week, I was on my way to New York.

In preparation for the all-important meeting, I posed this question during one of my quiet times: Do I bristle with confidence to gain the man's confidence? Or do I give him the details about the precariousness of my position and hope for his empathy?

The answer was to use humility.

"Mr. Robinson," I said, after he graciously invited me to lunch in one of the plush GM dining rooms, "you know why I'm here. What you *don't* know is that your answer will determine the success of a pioneering project—and possibly the fate of my career."

I then detailed the financial structure of my deal, told him how large companies were waiting for someone to make the first move, and how he could make or break the project.

"Somewhere in the dim past," I continued, "General Motors may have been in my position, looking for someone to take a chance on them. I now ask you to take a chance on me. Big fish should give little fish a chance to swim. That's what enlightened capitalism is all about, isn't it?"

He eyed me for a while. Then: "All you have going for you is your sincerity. All else is weak. However, I'm going to say yes, and you'd better not fail, or my superior will ask me why I led with my heart instead of my head. It's not often I use them in that order."

Within days after General Motors signed the lease, I placed a quarter-page ad in the *Milwaukee Journal* with this headline:

HERE ARE THE REASONS

WHY GENERAL MOTORS IS MOVING

TO 2040 WEST WISCONSIN AVENUE

Within a month, Prudential, Mutual of New York, Zurich, and a few others signed leases to move into my building. By the time the eight months were up, I had 75 percent of the unfinished structure leased. My cup was indeed running over.

My office building project became a huge financial success. After the debt service on the $3 million mortgage and all fixed expenses, I was left with a $150,000-a-year cash flow and a potential profit of $1.5 million in the event I decided to sell.

It was a major turning-point in my career, and with it came a flurry of insights for my life's value system. I was smitten with the creative aspect of the venture, its adventurous unknowns and their solutions. Had I invested my $500,000 in the stock market and earned $1.5 million within a matter of weeks, would I have experienced the same feeling of fulfillment as I did in building the office building? Never! I would have missed the joy of creativity.

All this led me to lock into an important insight: Risking to create usable wealth enriches society much more than playing the stock market. I felt the exhilaration of a double dividend: I had made a contribution to my community, and I did it as a locomotive, not a caboose—a pioneer, not a follower.

$ \qquad $ \$ \qquad \$ \qquad \$ \qquad \$ \qquad \$ \qquad \$

I HAD OFFERS to build office buildings in other cities but they didn't excite me. I wanted a different challenge. The locomotive-caboose analogy appealed to me. If I was to do another project, it had to be unusual, something that had not been done before. Just as a magnet attracts iron filings, so my mind soon attracted what I was looking for.

It was a 75-year-old, 100,000-square-foot, dust-laden warehouse, an eyesore that cast a shadow of neglect on a high-grade residential neighborhood a block away. What attracted my attention was that it was located two blocks from Lake Michigan and one block from St. Mary's Hospital. That gave me an idea. Why not convert it to a modern medical office building, from lowest to highest use—? I measured its appeal against my developing value system: it would meet doctors' needs because of its proximity to the hospital, it would resuscitate a dying building, and it would eliminate blight.

I bought the warehouse for $205,000 and plunged into the unknown. Converting an old structure into a modern medical building presented more problems than building a new one: the difficulty was to ascertain conversion costs, and thus the basis for a loan. There were no examples with which to make a comparison.

I decided on a bold plan of action. I negotiated with all my contractors on a price based on time and material with an agreed-upon margin of profit. It was a risky approach because costs could skyrocket out of control. But I had no choice.

Getting a loan on the basis of these unknown variables was formidable. I needed the ear of an unusual man. After many unsuccessful tries, I found him—Jim Gibson, a mortgage representative of the John Hancock Insurance Company.

After presenting all the salient selling points of my recycling project, I asked for an $850,000 mortgage based on a guess-timate cost of $1.1 million.

"If you're looking for a mortgage wrapped in blue ribbon safety," I told Gibson, "this is not it. It's an adventurous but prudent loan. In an adventure like this, what is needed is an imaginative mortgage man like you and a gutsy entrepreneur like me. Together we can do the unusual."

After three hours of intense negotiation, he agreed.

Getting tenants to sign leases when all I had to show was a windowless warehouse was fraught with uncertainties.

The Chief of Staff of St. Mary's Hospital, along with a group of four other surgeons, cautiously explored the possibility of moving their clinic to my building. As I anticipated, they liked being one block from their hospital, but they were hesitant about leasing space they had not seen.

"How do I know," the head doctor asked, "that our clinic will look as beautiful as your colored renderings?"

"I ask you to trust me, as I would trust you, if you were to operate on me."

He smiled, asked a few more questions, and signed the lease. Other doctors followed his lead.

Within a year, I had the building 100 percent occupied, with a rent roll of $240,000 a year. After fixed expenses and debt service on the $850,000 mortgage, I had a cash overage of $50,000 a year and a potential profit of $500,000.

I WAS AMAZED at my success. Was some invisible intelligence guiding me? As my sense of gratefulness increased, I began thinking seriously about God. Not the vague religious God of the synagogue, but the metaphysical mystery beyond.

I got a partial answer when I read *The Nazarene* by Sholem Asch. It transcended what I knew about Judaism and led me to the wisdom of the New Testament. My kindled new interest led to an experience that initiated a deluge of thinking far afield from real-estate venturing.

While on a family vacation trip to Mackinac Island, Michigan, I saw from a horse-drawn surrey a big sign reading MORAL RE-ARMAMENT. After my wife and three children were settled in their rooms at the Grand Hotel, I took a walk to investigate what was behind the sign.

When I knocked on the door of a large old rambling house, I was greeted by a young man who ushered me into a spacious living room overlooking Lake Michigan, where a dozen men and women were engaged in leisurely conversation. Friendly black, brown, and white faces turned to acknowledge me. A few were in native costumes of foreign countries. I was politely introduced by a gentleman with an English accent to people from Japan, France, Germany, Burma, and Kenya. After we talked and I told them a little about myself, the Englishman invited me to have breakfast with him the next morning.

"I want you to meet Dick, a former feature writer of a slick New York magazine. You'll not only find him interesting, you'll grasp through him what we're trying to do here."

After the three of us sat down for breakfast the next morning, Dick told the following story.

"My editor wanted a slick piece to show that Moral Re-Armament was a throwback to the Victorian Age. I holed up at the Grand Hotel with a couple of bottles of Scotch and began my interviews while an international MRA conference was in progress. For several days, the MRA people kept answering my cynical probes with a dignity that somehow began to blunt my cunning cleverness.''

"What particularly impressed you?'' I asked, my interest rising.

"They didn't quote the Bible. That attracted me.''

"Why?''

"Because the Bible had little meaning for me. My parents attended church only because it was the respectable thing to do, and their apathy spilled over on me. I was clever with words, so after I graduated from college, I got a job with a magazine. I got pretty good at it—and better still at profligacy, with booze leading the way. What else was there? I was accepted by my peers because they found me interesting. We were sophisticatedly nice to each other when it served our purposes, ruthless as hell when it didn't. When I came here to write the story about MRA, I found an environment so different from my own that I began to probe beyond my assignment.''

"What did you find?''

"*I found God*. It still sounds strange to say it, but that's the most direct way I can answer your question.''

"What did the MRA people say that your minister hadn't?''

"Something altogether different. They asked me to try an experiment.''

"What experiment?''

"They suggested that I remain quiet for an hour and listen to God before writing the article. It was an odd request—and for kicks, I thought I'd try it.''

"What happened?''

"For about twenty minutes my mind kept churning my usual manipulative thoughts. Then a brand new one began to move in. I began thinking about how genuine the MRA people were, and how phony I and my friends were. I compared the quiet elegance of the women I met at the MRA conference and the women I knew in New York—the clever ones with their mask of flashy fashion. It dawned on me that these people wanted nothing except to change me into a better person, while I was manipulating them to please my editor. I compared my selfish motives with theirs, my restlessness with their serenity, my drinking with their clear-eyed freedom, my drift from pleasure to pleasure to their joy of raising the quality of their lives and helping others do the same. As these thoughts crossed and re-crossed my mind, I began to suspect that perhaps this is the way God talks to us—when we listen quietly."

"What happened next?" I asked, with rising curiosity.

"When I told a few of the MRA people what went through my mind during my quiet time, a banker who was among them said, 'Now that you listened and God has spoken, the only logical thing for you to do is obey.' "

"You're here," I said. "You must have obeyed."

"Yes, after several sessions of quiet times," he continued, "I began to obey and change—slowly at first, faster as the enormity of my change began to fill my consciousness. I came to stay a few days. I stayed six weeks. I went back to New York without the story, but a changed man."

"I've so many questions," I said, "that I don't know where to begin. Let me start with this one: Have you dropped out of your church?"

"No, but I don't find it as relevant as my new church."

"What new church?"

"The uncodified one I find in the privacy of my quiet time."

On further questioning, I found that the Moral Re-Armament movement was not a religious cult, but an international bonding of people who were looking for a common-denominator spiritually to raise the quality of their lives. To guide their change, they strived to measure their lives against four absolute standards: absolute honesty, unselfishness, purity, and love. And from what I've seen, they really work at it.

I was seeing a new breed of man—a Mau-Mau terrorist from Kenya who changed into a disciplined man, a Communist from Italy who began to believe in God for the first time, a go-go girl from Sweden who changed into a modern Mary Magdalene. After mingling with these revolutionarily changed people from some twenty different countries with varied religions, cultures and races, my mind was filled with new perceptions. Heretofore, I was acquainted with orthodox Judaism and a smattering of Christianity. These people were not satisfied with their prescribed religions; they were more interested in acquiring the wisdom to remove religious barriers and build bridges of universal spiritual understanding.

This new thinking gripped my interest. The people I met fascinated me—so different from those I dealt with in Milwaukee. My mind buzzed with doubt: Where was reality? In Milwaukee or what I found on Mackinac Island? It took several weeks before I settled back into my comfortable business groove. But a residual unease remained. Could all these intelligent men and women be reaching for pie in the sky—or was their way the spiritual wave of the future? I decided to test my interest by comparing it with the opinions of some of my intelligent friends.

I got four men to accompany me on four separate occasions to Mackinac Island: John Butcher, president of a bank; Abel Berland, president of Rubloff company, the largest real-estate company in Chicago; Dr. Richard Weil, a psychology professor; and Lawrence Katz, Federal Housing Administrator of Wisconsin. None of them was as excited about MRA as I was, but their lack of enthusiasm didn't diminish mine. My thinking and my work had been touched in a very practical way.

MRA   MRA   MRA   MRA   MRA

IN 1960 a 70-year-old woman, who had been one of my favorite high-school teachers, came to my office and, after a few pleasantries, said:

"George, I know there's more money building for the rich insurance companies than building housing for the elderly.

But don't you think that, after working hard all our lives, we deserve housing suited to our retirement needs?"

Somewhat sheepishly I replied, "To be frank, Mrs. Witte, I've been so busy with my new office building that I hadn't given it any thought; but I will now. I vividly remember how you helped me. Perhaps now I can help you."

My Moral Re-Armament idealism welled up a selfless motivation that transcended my profit goal. I knew there was no money in building for the elderly, but didn't I have a moral obligation to put some of my building experience where the need was most urgent? Had I not been exposed to the MRA experience, I probably would have passed up my promise to Mrs. Witte. But what I had witnessed on Mackinac Island drew me into a new realm of thinking. I felt something new—sparks of inspiration.

I bought a three-acre site overlooking the Milwaukee River in a park-like setting. I drew plans for 94 apartments with special amenities for the elderly that had never been offered before —a large meeting room, a library, a small restaurant for the exclusive use of the golden-agers and their visiting children and grandchildren, a hobby shop, prayer room, shuffleboard courts, and the most desirable amenity of all: an outdoor patio for each apartment. An artist drew a color rendering of a rambling white-brick, two-story colonial structure, showing the patios trimmed with black corrugated iron railings, against a backdrop of lush green trees and the blue Milwaukee River.

Armed with this effective selling piece and a meticulously structured pro-forma statement of income, fixed expenses, and cost of construction, I set out to obtain a $500,000 mortgage. I was turned down by a half-dozen Savings and Loan Associations for two main reasons: elderly people are not good rent risks, and the $75,000 allocated for the special amenities was not income-producing.

The uniqueness of the project fired my interest and kept it burning. I was determined to see it through. During one of my quiet times, the thought came to me that since the project was spiritually conceived, it might have to be spiritually financed. How? Who? One thought triggered another. What about Al Kliebon, my Catholic-fundamentalist mortgage-banker friend? I called him the same morning.

"Al, I've got a problem that only you can solve. Can I see you?"

"Any time," came the cordial reply.

He listened and smiled as I detailed my concept and then told him about all my turn-downs.

"We mortgage bankers have to protect other people's money when we approve loans," he said. "You were turned down because the lenders weren't sure that older people want to live together. Also, retired tenants have little money, and they're not earners. *I'll* have to turn you down, George, for the same reasons. Don't blame *me*. Doing Caesar's work is part of my job."

"How about doing God's work?" My pent-up frustration burst at being turned down by a devout Catholic.

"What do you mean?"

"This is a special project which deserves special risk. It's more than a commercial loan. It's a way of helping the elderly who've worked hard all their lives and now want to spend their remaining years in an affordable, beautiful environment. Look, I'm risking $250,000 in cash against your $500,000 mortgage. My risk is much greater than yours. I can be wiped out, and you could end up owning a $750,000 project for $500,000. So much for *Caesar's* security. What about the old folks' security?"

I could see he was moved.

"George, let me see what I can do. You'll hear from me."

Several weeks later he called. "George, you've got the loan. I've gone out of my way, and I want you to do the same to make it a success. It's never been done before, and the eyes of the community will be on us. We'd better not fail."

Riverwood, the name I chose for the project, was successful

from many angles—architecturally, commercially, spiritually. Retired schoolteachers, firemen, secretaries, widows, widowers, and elderly couples left their homes and apartments and flocked to the resort-like environment of Riverwood. The special amenities added a social dimension to their lives.

To make it affordable for low-income retired people, I structured the rent 30 percent below market—$138 for a one-bedroom unit and $152 for a two-bedroom unit.

It was far below the profitability of my office building project, but what a difference in inspirational rewards! When my wife and I joined the tenants occasionally in some of their social activities in the recreation area overlooking the forest-clad Milwaukee River, many would bless us profusely for what we'd done for their lives. Several sent poems expressing their appreciation. We even got several wedding invitations from golden-aged couples whose romances started at Riverwood.

Whenever I needed a change from my busily scheduled real-estate office, I would leave for Riverwood to spend a few hours with its happy tenants.

THE HEARTWARMING SUCCESS of Riverwood gave a new slant to my real-estate business. It involved meeting the needs of people in tandem with keeping an eye on the bottom line. This new mode of thinking and doing brought me closer to pioneering with a purpose. My mind looked for such a venture and a door opened.

I bought a two-hundred-unit converted apartment building that had formerly been used as a hotel. It was a uniquely charming structure overlooking Lake Michigan with quality architecture and a lobby that oozed with Old-World nostalgia. Despite these assets, it was half empty and the owners were losing money. When I bought the building, I had a gut feeling that it had a lot of potential for a pioneering use, but at the time I didn't know for what.

In one of my quiet times, I posed this question: If a person is over 80 years old, mobile and healthy enough not to need a nursing home, but too feeble to live alone in a big house or apartment, where should he or she live?

No one had ever tried to fill this need, and that gave me the additional impetus to do it. It was risky—financially and managerially.

That uncertainty only spurred me on.

I converted three adjoining apartments into a charming small restaurant, exclusively for octogenarians and beyond, and began advertising for elderly tenants. I offered a small apartment, switchboard security, a nurse on the premises, a part-time social director, and three meals a day—all for $350 a month for a single, and $550 for a couple in a larger apartment.

Within one year I leased seventy apartments to widows, widowers, and couples ranging in age from 80 to 100. They came from physicians' recommendations in cases where the extreme elderly had no choice but to live alone, from children's homes where both were uncomfortable, and from nursing homes where they had to live alongside the very sick when all they needed was the minimal care I provided to maintain their independence. Several lonely and formerly wealthy businessmen and socialite women came to live at the Knickerbocker, as it was called, not for the low rental, but because there was no better alternative to meet their desire for safe, independent living.

As I was increasing my advertising to fill the 200 apartments with the very elderly, a social worker from the Department of Health, Education, and Welfare visited the Knickerbocker and, although impressed with what she saw, cautioned, "Don't make the mistake of filling the entire building with seniors. Don't institutionalize them. If you want to prolong their independence, put them in the mainstream with younger people. I'd suggest only one-third of the units for the elderly."

She was a wise woman who knew more than I about the psychological needs of those over 80. I took her through my River-wood Apartments, where the average age was between 65 and 75. On the way out she said with a smile, "These are your 'swingers'; they're still in the mainstream. But the ones at the Knickerbocker are 'survivors'—they need young tenants for companionship."

I took her advice.

In order to provide youthful mainstream companionship for my "survivors," I got another idea during one morning's quiet time. I would lease apartments by the week or month and call the arrangement Home Away From Home.

Within a year, aided by innovative advertising and pro-motion, the Knickerbocker became a home-away-from-home for short-stay executives, visiting professors, trainees, etc. It was used by local people who were dislodged by fire, husbands who were cooling off after arguments with their wives, and families who either had to wait before getting into houses they had bought or had to get out on a certain date after selling their homes.

The very elderly now had opportunities to mingle and make friends with the ever-changing, interesting people who, in turn, enjoyed the elderly as much as the elderly enjoyed them. The unusual idea of blending the old with the young created a uniquely compatible combination.

My aim of blending the needs of people with making a profit worked perfectly at the Knickerbocker. After taking two years to fill it, and three years of operation, it showed a cash flow of $75,000 a year after all fixed expenses and debt service on a $1.5 million mortgage. I sold it for a $500,000 profit.

ﾵ $ ﾵ $ ﾵ $ ﾵ

MY SUCCESSFUL VENTURES were reported in the Milwaukee Jour-nal, and neophyte entrepreneurs called me and asked how they could get into deals like mine with little money.

About the same time, I got a request from the University of Wisconsin Education Outreach to teach a course in real estate. I agreed to seventeen weeks, two hours a week on Wednesday evenings from seven to nine. The brochure announced my course with this unusual title: "How to Get into Big Real Estate Deals with Little Money."

I watched with a great deal of curiosity as the "students" filed in for my first lecture. Most wore their working clothes and looked weary after their day's work. There were about fifty in the room, with an average age of between 35 and 50. I spent a lot of time preparing for my teaching stint because I wanted to make a practical difference in their lives.

I started off by calling their attention to the four prerequisites for a successful real-estate entrepreneur—guts, imagination, persuasion, and integrity—and explained each one in detail. I then zeroed in on what they came to hear—concrete examples on how to get into deals with little or no money. To gain their attention, I described how I got into a $500,000 deal without a dime of my own money. As weary as they were, I perked most of them up with the following story:

"An elderly man owned an 80,000-square-foot building on the northwest corner of Seventh and Wisconsin avenues. It was formerly used as an automobile agency and was now half empty. He was collecting $40,000 annual rent and his expenses were about the same. But he was asking $500,000 for it because it was located on Wisconsin Avenue, Milwaukee's main street. He had been trying to sell it for several years with no takers.

"This was my proposal to him: You lease the building to me for 50 years on the basis of a $500,000 value, capitalized at a 4 percent interest, or $20,000 a year. This is $20,000 a year more than you are getting now. If you sold it for $500,000, which you can't, and paid $200,000 in income taxes, you would be left with $300,000, which, invested at the prevailing 4 percent interest, would only net you $12,000 a year. In *my* plan, you get $20,000 a year free of all encumbrances.

"Price-wise, return-wise, and tax-wise, it makes a lot of sense to accept my offer, doesn't it? But it would not be a mutually good deal unless this plan also made sense for me. It does, and I'll tell you why. I can fill your half-empty building and make a profit for my work. It's a double win. We both gain.

"After several hours of negotiating and a few days with his lawyers, we closed the deal, and I became the owner of a $500,000 asset without a dime of my money. Within a year, I got the rent up to $80,000 by spending $100,000 upgrading it with the money from a $100,000 mortgage. I realized a cash flow of $20,000 a year after fixed expenses and the lease rental of $20,000. I eventually sold my leasehold equity for $150,000. So you see, it's possible to get into real-estate deals with little or no money."

During the weeks that followed, I explained variations on the theme of getting into deals with little or no money. I could tell that my practical examples were keeping the tired working-men awake.

%   %   %   %   %   %

THE SEVENTEEN-WEEK real-estate course proved to be a huge success for me and my students. I was enjoying sharing my knowledge, and they were making deals as a result of our discussions. Two outstanding examples gave me a special good feeling.

One involved a 39-year-old electrician who came to class in his working cap, with black dirt under his fingernails. I described the physical features of a 24-family apartment, emphasizing its decrepit condition. The elderly owner, I added, was tired of his managerial problems and was anxious to sell it on easy terms. It was a perfect deal for a handyman with no money.

The electrician walked up to my desk at the end of the session and said:

"I'd like to buy it. I qualify—I'm a handyman with no money. But I have guts, imagination, and lots of integrity. I just lack persuasion. If you could persuade a bank to loan me $40,000 like you explained, I would like to take a chance. I'm familiar with the building."

I profiled the deal as follows: Asking-price: $220,000; first mortgage: $120,000; second mortgage: $60,000; and cash-down payment: $40,000.

I introduced Bob Prittchet to John Butcher, president of American City Bank, who qualified him for the $40,000 loan. Within one year, Bob, his wife, and son rejuvenated the twenty-four apartments and doubled the rents. Two years later, armed with the confidence of success, he bought a group of vacant buildings adjoining his apartment—an old theater, eight stores, a garage, and a lot—for $350,000, with a $50,000 down-payment. The seller was a multimillion-dollar New York real-estate company that was eager to get rid of its losing out-of-town properties. Bob's family and relatives recycled the "junk" vacant buildings and filled them with tenants.

Now, eighteen years later, Bob owns all the property free and clear, and nets $150,000 a year after all expenses. He'll retire in grand style—the outgrowth of attending a night course in real-estate.

Another dramatic example of getting into a big deal with little money was restaurateur George Pandl, who, with $10,000 down, now owns a restaurant worth $1.5 million. It was a case of two needs coming into juxtaposition. A rich playboy bought a restaurant for $300,000 and, not knowing much about the business, was losing $75,000 a year. After two years, he called me and said, "George, get me out of this. I don't belong here!"

At about the same time, George Pandl, who heard about my course on getting into big deals with little money, came to my office and said, "Mr. Bockl, I'm an excellent chef with a crew of six grown children who can run a good-sized restaurant, but I have no money. Can you help me?"

I got George to scrape up $10,000 from friends and relatives, I helped him get a $150,000 first mortgage on the building and fixtures, a second mortgage of $90,000 from the owner, and sold him the restaurant for $250,000. George is now retired in a beautiful home on Lake Michigan and his son Jim is running the restaurant, grossing $2 million a year in sales.

THESE TWO EXAMPLES, and others, added an important building block to my developing value structure. It was this: Giving creates goodwill, getting begets discord. When I was giving my knowledge to Bob Prittchet and George Pandl, there was a harmonious feeling between us, but when I was getting a loan or ambitiously pursuing a tenant, the harmonious vibrations were not quite there. Dissonance usually replaced pleasantness.

But getting is a function of life, and the challenge I faced was not to let it run amok, but to idealize it into friendly mutuality instead of confrontational aggressiveness.

I had an opportunity to see at close range what happens to ultra-successful tycoons who fall prey to letting uncontrolled getting run their lives. I was asked to introduce the dean of America's real-estate developers at the time to a group of Milwaukee realtors and city officials. I was intimidated at the prospect of handling the lion of our business, reputed to own $200 million worth of hotels, office buildings, apartment complexes, and regional shopping centers. What I had heard about him was that he was as ruthless as he was astute, likened to a runaway truck without brakes, demolishing all obstacles that got in his way.

After his talk, I had a chance to visit him in his hotel room. It confirmed what I had heard. He was cold, impersonal, and unfriendly. I had the feeling he regarded me as some small-town yokel. I, in turn, saw a man whose obsessive getting turned him into a machine. His eyes were looking at me, but not his mind.

It was churning beyond my presence. Whatever temptation I had to get into big-time real-estate deals began evaporating. My giving/getting theory took on new significance. The frenzied getters, I ruminated, lose far more than they win, and the majority don't know it.

What finally stopped the siren ringing in my ears about getting into multimillion-dollar deals was an encounter with the biggest real-estate developer in Chicago, Arthur Rubloff. I was introduced to him by Abel Berland, my very good friend, who was president of the Rubloff Company.

I was ushered into a huge, art-filled, luxurious office where the immaculately dressed Mr. Rubloff greeted me in a suave, smileless manner. Without any small-talk preliminaries, he launched into a description of a real-estate investment trust (REIT) deal that was a popular vehicle for going public at that time.

"This is a good time," he began, "to take advantage of the REIT-going-public craze. I can get your income-producing properties appraised for $10 million. That, after your $5 million of mortgages, will give you a $5 million equity position. I own a prime site of 200 acres outside Boston that is ripe for a regional shopping center, which will appraise for $3 million. I'll throw in another $2 million worth of land to match your $5 million to make us 50/50 partners. We'll then sell 50 percent of our stock to the public for $10 million and split $5 million in cash between us. Your real estate will provide the bread-and-butter income for our deal, and my shopping-center site for future growth. It'll be a balanced real-estate portfolio. And if the REIT takes off, as I know it will, we could make another $5 million apiece for each of our 25 percent interest. What do you say?"

For a moment he dropped his suavity. His eyes gleamed and his voice crackled with excitement.

I did a lot of thinking while driving home from Chicago—about the man and the deal. I knew instinctively that I would not want to emulate him, even if I could have the $100 million he was reputed to be worth. I had explored myself enough to know that it was not a case of sour grapes or a holier-than-thou attitude. It was the fact that he oozed the same negative vibrations the dean of real estate did, cold and calculating—a different kind of man than those I met on Mackinac Island in Moral Re-Armament.

I wondered if the zealous drive to *get* imperceptibly creates the tendencies toward manipulation and ruthlessness. Perhaps their genius drives some men relentlessly in one direction because they just don't take the time to explore the big picture—putting purpose into their lives.

Was I too judgmental? What about all the good Rubloff contributed to society? He built the Miracle Mile on Michigan Avenue, Sandberg Village, and other projects that created thousands of jobs. Wasn't he a man of action, a builder of wealth? And when he died, what about the $60 million he left to charity? Wasn't he a mixture of good and bad? The experience got me thinking toward a new frontier, the challenge of combining the creation of wealth with making a contribution—a far more elusive goal than mere capitalistic venturing.

As a starter, I turned down Rubloff's deal.

5

AT THE EDGE OF A PATHLESS UNKNOWN

Religions Did Not Provide the Open,
Boundless Spiritual Values
I Was Looking For.

WHILE I WAS BALANCING MY BUSINESS AND pro-bono work, a personal tragedy struck me with shocking suddenness. My 20-year-old son, Bob, was killed in an automobile accident. The terrible blow pierced my heart with grief and paralyzed my mind.

My close-knit family would never be the same again. My wife and two older daughters and I were jolted out of our normal happy life. Our minds refused to accept the reality that nothing would ever be the same. Just when I was beginning to enjoy Bob's developing sensitivity and maturity, he was gone! And my plans to nurture his career and have him succeed me—they were gone too! A dark emptiness filled my mind. I felt and thought of nothing except the intense pain of Bob's death.

The usual, well-intentioned condolences did not assuage our affliction, except for one. It came from a tenant in my building who was a member of a small group who called themselves Theosophists. It read:

"Your son has not died into oblivion. He lives on another level of existence where he's assimilating his earthly experiences, after which he will be born again to build on what he has learned from his previous incarnations. His permanent, individualized Spark of God within him will take your son through eons of incarnations, each one urging him to process his physical experiences into spiritual wisdom. All of us are on a never-ending journey, with different life-spans in different incarnations, but always evolving onward into eternity. Your son's future is assured in the immortal law of everlasting life.''

The content of the letter gave me some solace. I reread it many times. What if it were true—that death is but a recurring incident in an endless life in a continually evolving experience—? But the hope soon evaporated. The dark cloud of my loss blanketed my mind again. I lost interest in my work, in my pro-bono giving, and in Moral Re-Armament. The inspiration stopped bubbling.

For several years my business was in limbo and my mind in deep doldrums. During those sad days, the optimistic promise of the Theosophical message kept flickering in my mind until it ignited an interest to pursue it.

I learned that the Theosophical Society was composed of people worldwide in some 75 countries, belonging to any religion or none, who were united to remove religious antagonisms and draw together men and women of goodwill, whatever their religious opinions. Their bond of union was not the profession of a common belief, but a common search for Truth. They regarded truth as a prize to be striven for, not as a dogma to be imposed by authority. They stressed individual study and the development of faith based on knowledge, not clerical assertion.

As I dug deeper into Theosophical literature, I found three cardinal principles upon which its philosophy rested:

1. There exists an Absolute, out of which emerged the Cosmic Intelligence or God that powers the Universe.

2. This Cosmic Intelligence or Energy, using the law of evolution, constantly constructs, destroys, and regenerates

universes, galaxies, and solar systems, including every-
thing that has cyclical life.

3. Man is within this system of cyclical periodicity, evolving toward the Originating Source or God through eons of
physical incarnations.

Not being of a scholarly nature, my reaction to these new
ideas was more confusion than relief, and combined with the
stagnation of my work and the wound of my son's loss, my
body began to wilt. I lost weight and energy, and I developed
stomach pains. I was tested by local doctors and at the Mayo
Clinic. They found no organic reasons for my illness. I tossed
about for answers, and none came until I met a Christian
Scientist. My life took a radical turn as I plunged into learning
the difference between mortal mind and divine Mind.

MY DEBILITATING HEALTH problem caused my life's agenda to fade
in importance. Whether my ailing body disturbed my mind, or
my disturbed mind caused my illness, was the chicken-and-egg
dilemma that the doctors couldn't fathom. The subsequent confusion aggravated the agitation of both mind and body.

I wasn't as concerned about neglecting my business as I was
in my inability to pursue my awakened interest in a Theosophical God. Discouragement set in—something I hadn't
experienced in years. When a friend of mine suggested I ought
to look into Christian Science, I was distressed enough to
grasp at it.

When I walked into a Wednesday evening Christian Science
service, an usher met me at the door and courteously escorted
me to a few rows in front of the lectern. I found myself in a
large, well-lit, plain room that looked more like an auditorium
than a church.

At eight o'clock sharp, a middle-aged man approached the lecturn from a side door. He read several passages from the Bible, followed by passages from another book that I later learned was *Science and Health with Key to the Scriptures*, by Mary Baker Eddy, the discoverer and founder of Christian Science. The audience sang several hymns, after which the man said:

"I now invite you to share your testimonies and remarks on Christian Science healing."

After several people in the congregation got up and told how they were cured of arthritis, bladder inflammation, eczema, and ulcers, the reader announced his desire to conclude the evening service with his own story.

"While I was a junior in college," he began, "I was afflicted with cancer of the esophagus. Doctors gave me little hope. I hit the bottom rung of despair. My family and my Episcopal pastor looked on helplessly. I quit school.

"A classmate of mine suggested that I see a Christian Science practitioner. I was skeptical, but desperate. I went to see one. When I finished relating my problem, the practitioner looked at me serenely and, without a trace of alarm, said, 'There's no disease divine Mind can't heal.' Then he added, speaking with authority, 'Divine Mind is the most powerful, the most scientific healing agent known to man, provided it is not merely believed, but understood. Understanding is the key; and diligently studying *Science and Health* will give you that understanding.'

"I bought the book and immersed myself in its beautiful prose, hardheaded logic, and, above all, its convincing arguments how switching from mortal mind to divine Mind creates a radical change in mind and body. I read and reread the chapter on 'Fruitage'—the dozens of concrete healing examples. They sounded miraculous at the time; but what sounds miraculous to mortal mind is natural to divine Mind. After I finished reading the book and attending several months of Sunday and Wendesday services, fear and worry left me, and with them the symptoms of cancer. My health was completely restored. This happened twenty years ago, and I haven't stopped expressing my gratitude to Christian Science ever since."

I asked the man at my side for the speaker's name. The next day I was in Gordon Smith's office. After a few preliminaries, I asked:

"Tell me specifically how you changed from mortal mind to divine Mind. It seems to be the centerpiece of your healing."

"I stand guard at the gate of mind and turn back the fears and worries that used to churn my insides, which eventually exploded into cancer."

"Am I to conclude that by your guarding against negative thoughts, divine Mind takes over and you become a radically different person?"

"You've got it. It's an exciting, daily challenge, an unritual-ized religion that propels you faster toward God's ways because you don't have the rite and rote to slow you down."

My friendship with Gordon resulted in my reading Mary Baker Eddy's *Science and Health*, attending several dozen Sunday and Wednesday evening services, and joining a Friday noon luncheon group where Christian Scientists from several churches in the city met at the Milwaukee Athletic Club.

Gordon, of course, was always among them, gracing the table with his joyous wit and pleasant effervescence. While most of the other diners in the large room were smoking, drinking, and conversing loudly, the Scientists' quiet joy was a serene contrast to the raucousness of their neighbors.

Gordon's spiritual thoughts and friendship increased my strength and decreased by stomach's squeamishness. My interest in business and my pursuit of a new and different religious feeling were revived. My body stopped complaining and my mind cleared of anxiety. I was healed! Was it because I took Gordon's advice and used his picturesque phrase to stand guard at the portal of my mind, allowing only healthy thoughts to enter and keeping out the fearful ones? Or did whatever was wrong with me wear out and return my body to normality? I credited the first.

Christian Science soothed my mind and removed anxieties. Its wisdom spurred me on to look further. What if there were something even more profound than Moral Re-Armament, Theosophy, or Christian Science? What if there were some super-wisdom that combined these three and others into one essential, universal spirituality? What if there were some challenge greater than success, more exciting than real-estate venturing? A murmuring began in my blood. Energized by my new found health, I decided to investigate.

WHEN A FRIEND OF MINE suggested that I should explore Unitarianism, I quickly agreed—because of its very name.

Accompanied by my friend, Jack, a Unitarian, I walked into what looked more like a lecture hall than a chapel. There was no religious art, not even a cross. The people in the audience were well dressed, and as I scrutinized faces, I had the feeling that they were also well educated. After the congregation sang several hymns, an impeccably dressed, gray-haired man walked up to the pulpit.

"He's one of the most successful industrialists in the city," Jack whispered.

"I'm a practical businessman," the speaker began. "I seek a rational rather than an emotional approach to God. I'm here because my common sense tells me that all religions are essentially the same. They stress the same virtues and fall prey to the same vices. They stress love, but divide themselves with hate. Unitarianism is an attempt to loosen dogmatic thinking, to cross religious boundaries, to seek parallel wisdoms and not to be trapped into divisiveness. I use insights from many sources to improve my business. Why not seek God in the same way?''

The minister ended the service not with a sermon, but with a talk on the need for United World Federalism.

''The universe operates with precision based on laws laid down by a Universal Intelligence. Our efforts to live by law is reflective of that Universal Law. After centuries of struggle, we've reached a point in evolution where a person cannot impose his will upon another without being confronted by law. Yet a nation, if it's strong enough, can impose its will on another with impunity. Why? Because nations are still living in a legal jungle, threatening and bullying each other as did primitive man.''

I was puzzled by the secular content of the talk.

''In the absence of international laws,'' the minister continued, ''countries solve their differences by war. They've tried treaties and power politics, but these have only delayed the organized violence. Without enforceable law, personal relationships beween people would be in shambles. As long as there's no enforceable world law, relationships between nations will remain as they are today—primitive. Our chance for greatness does not lie in exploring the moon. America's greatness lies in developing a United World Federation backed by world law and a world army, so that countries can be civilized the way individuals are civilized—by law. The world can no longer afford the luxury of an American dream, or a Russian dream— it must be a world dream.''

I began to wonder what all this had to do with religion. The answer came when the minister concluded:

''Religion should have a double approach: individual growth and societal welfare. I would give priority to the first, only if it accelerates the good works of the second. They are mutually reciprocal.''

I attended many Unitarian services during the next several

months and did a lot of thinking. I discussed my views with Jack, who was a devout Unitarian.

"What's so attractive about Unitarianism that keeps you so interested?"

"It combines faith with action. For instance, building a United World Federation, defusing nuclear warheads, promoting civil rights—this is religion at its finest."

"It's social activism. It has its place—but it's not religion."

"Unitarianism balances other-worldliness with this-worldliness. Each reinforces the other."

Jack did not convince me, nor did the Unitarian services. They concentrated on secular matters. I was looking for a spiritual wisdom that combined what I had learned in Moral Re-Armament, Theosophy, and Christian Science—some gripping idea that would answer my nagging question: what's beyond success? I didn't find it in Unitarianism.

? ? ? ? ? ? ?

DOUBTS BEGAN TO CREEP IN. Was I seeking something that couldn't be found beyond rite and rote? Were these needed to shore up interest in an ultimate ideal? Were charismatic clergy an indispensable aid? Without these things, would the bulk of humanity dissipate into a spiritless void? Confusion was nipping at my mind.

To add fuel to my skepticism, my Jewish friends and relatives began peppering me with questions and subtle condemnations. "Isn't Judaism good enough for you?" "If you paid more attention to the wisdom of your own faith, you wouldn't be wasting your time on others." "If you don't stand for something, you stand for nothing!" " You're all over the lot with your naive probing."

I countered with what I found in the broader-based wisdom of Moral Re-Armament, Theosophy, and Christian Science. They had a wider vision than any closed religious system; there was a greater challenge in actively probing spiritual knowledge than having it served up by tradition and digested by clergy's literalism.

Had I been a failure, or some business nonentity, my friends in and out of Judaism would have tossed me aside as a dilettante, an oddity, and left me alone. But because I was a success and gave lavishly to Jewish and Gentile charities, community leaders didn't know where to pigeonhole me.

I overcame the problem by not expressing my views unless someone showed a genuine interest. Very few did, and I merrily went on with my business and they with theirs. But on a deeper level, it bothered me. If I kept my new spiritual thinking bottled up, how would it spread? How would the old ever change into the new?

Proselytizing was anathema to me. I viewed my quest as a personal journeying into the Unknown with the same pioneering spirit as I had venturing into pioneering real estate. Though I didn't have the learning capacity of a scholar or theologian, I nevertheless felt confident that I could chart my own evolutionary path. Because I could depend on my balanced, logical nature, I was not concerned about veering off into some stagnant cul-de-sac or grotesque cult.

I knew there was danger in leaving the trodden path, but there was also intrigue in creating my own. Ralph Waldo Emerson expressed it better: "Do not go where the path may lead; go instead where there is no path and leave a trail."

I was alone in my pursuit, but not lonely. I rendered to my business its due diligence, and equal diligence to my spiritual quest. I managed to keep my inner and outer lives in balance.

ॐ   ॐ   ॐ   ॐ   ॐ   ॐ

ALTHOUGH SEVERAL UNUSUAL real-estate ventures were nibbling at my mind, I put them on hold while I continued to investigate other religions. I had read some of Buddhism's complex literature, but not much had rubbed off. But I was intrigued enough to look up a devotee while on a vacation trip to Hawaii. He was a Buddhist monk who had given up his Methodist ministry for Buddhism's wisdom.

"The formal Methodist religion of which I was a part," he said when we met, "had a closed system of belief, while Buddhism has no frontiers and is not in opposition to any religion. It's open-endedly creative and does not die through repetition."

When I asked him how God is viewed in his religion, he replied that no world teacher was as godless as the Buddha, yet few more godlike.

"What was his essential message that changed hundreds of millions to his way of teaching?" I asked.

"His main message was that the cause of human suffering comes from too much desire—thoughtless cravings, sensual cravings, power, and possessions."

"Did the Buddha tell his followers how to get rid of human suffering?"

"Yes—by what he called the Eightfold Path leading to extinction of desire: right understanding, right mindedness, right speech, right action, right living, right effort, right attentiveness, and right concentration."

"What you've explained so far," I said, "merely refines and institutionalizes secular humanism. I'm trying to understand the difference between a religious God and a spiritual God. You've changed from a religious God to a human God."

I came away from the question-and-answer meeting informed, but not transformed.

I realized that I had been exposed only to a surface knowledge of Buddhism. But my quest didn't urge me to an in-depth study of it. My aim was to obtain a feel for the various religions, and if any one grabbed me, I'd follow it wherever it led. Buddhism didn't quicken me. It was more intellectual than spiritual. Undaunted in not finding a spiritual vision to excite my heart, I doggedly kept up my quest.

?   !   ?   !   ?   !

MY PERSONAL KNOWLEDGE about the Baha'i faith came from a Jewish business associate, Jack Lee, who married a follower of the faith. After attending several Baha'i meetings and many discussions with Jack and his wife, I learned that the essence of their faith was what they called progressive revelation. God, from time to time, inspires prophets to provide new spiritual teachings to advance humanity's development. Each succeeding prophet confirms the validity of the previous ones. Baha' Ullah , who founded the Baha'i faith in the 1860s, is the prophet of our time, he claimed, after a series of prophets, beginning with Adam and continuing through the lives of Jewish prophets, Jesus, and Muhammad.

Baha' Ullah's new revelations that transcended those of the previous prophets were: individual search for truth, the equality of men and women, the harmony of science and religion, the need for world government, and the preservation of cultural diversity.

"Has it made any headway since Baha' Ullah began his preaching?" I asked Arden, Jack's wife.

With the enthusiasm of a devotee, she cited the following: There are about 110,000 chapters in 132 countries; about 1700 tribes have representation in the faith; and Baha'i literature has been translated into 650 dialects and languages.

"Does that give you some idea of the headway we're making?" she asked proudly.

But the Baha'i faith didn't make any headway with me. The people I met within the faith were middle-class, intelligent, but boxed in by their devotion to Baha' Ullah. I was looking for a relationship with God without intermediaries.

The most significant mark it left on me was that Arden was able to convert my Jewish associate to the Baha'i faith instead of the other way around.

"For me," Jack said at lunch one day, "the Baha'i faith is

both the oldest and newest religion, as old as the first prophet, and as new as Baha' Ullah.''

It satisfied him, but not me.

I CORNERED MY MIND to answer the question that had been vexing me in my search. Why was I doing it? Weren't a happy family life and a super-successful business enough? The vast majority don't search; why do I? They seem to lead normal, happy lives. Why can't I? My logical mind countered: If I deviated from orthodox real-estate venturing with remarkable results, why not deviate from the ''orthodox'' in venturing to find something *big* to live for? Wasn't that far more important?

There was another reason. Whatever drove me to explore the world in books when I became literate now fueled my interest to explore the Invisible Reality, or God—the focus of yearnings for hundreds of millions. To my way of thinking, I had chosen an interest that was far more ultimate than amassing wealth, collecting art, or any pursuit that merely satisfied the intellect.

A FRIEND OF MINE who was acquainted with my quest suggested that I read a book by J. Krishnamurti. He described the author as the most revolutionary spiritual philosopher of the twentieth century. I read the book and was so entranced that I persuaded my wife to fly with me to Ojai, California, where Krishnamurti was giving a series of lectures.

About 1000 people had gathered on a grassy clearing surrounded by a grove of oak trees to hear the 80-year-old's radical views on how to transform today's society. He sat on a chair behind a bare table on a slightly raised wooden platform. Some in the audience were standing, others reclined on blankets they had brought along. A warm mountain breeze added a fragrant freshness to the scene. Except for a few curious newcomers, most were familiar with Krishnamurti's provocative ideas.

Some of his radical views were completely new to me. It took a lot of quiet time thinking, and reading a dozen of his books, to reconcile his spiritual logic with what I had absorbed heretofore. Here are excerpts from Krishnamurti's views:

The unquestioned, fossilized religious beliefs have caused much of the world's misery.

Devotion is not a virtue. The sages of the ages apotheosized it. The holy scriptures glorified it. Yet, devotion followed to its logical conclusion is not a virtue, but a vice. Why? Because intense dedication to a religion leads to prejudice, proselytizing, and violence.

Holiness! A virtue? Not at all! Look at all the havoc it's caused as the holiness of one religion clashes with the sacredness of another. The religious leaders dogmatize at the top and divide mankind at the bottom.

Tradition! A great virtue? No! A dangerous vice! The Wailing Wall in Jerusalem, and Mecca in Saudi Arabia, are hallowed symbols of tradition that have led to religious divisions and violence. Tradition dulls, narrows, and clamps minds into straight-jackets.

Ambition! It has warped men into egotism and insensitivity. It's been overmerchandised to the detriment of its worshippers and the sorrow of its victims. At the end of unbridled ambition is a hollow abyss.

Krishnamurti's quicksilverish views were more than revolutionary. They jarred the very foundations of Western culture. I was intrigued and confused. I saw several profound truths, but they receded as I tried to grasp them. Because I couldn't agree or disagree with his ideas, I decided to let them float in my mind without any destination.

6

WHAT'S BEYOND SUCCESS?

*It Was Inconceivable That There Would Not Be
a More Ultimate Challenge Than
Financial Success.*

M Y DELVING INTO THE VARIOUS RELIGIONS DID
not arouse a gripping feeling for God—not the way
it must resonate in the hearts and minds of devoted
fundamentalists. It took several months to pacify myself with
the balm that if I couldn't find an engrossing ideal in other-
worldliness, perhaps I could find it in this-worldliness—in the
secular realm. Didn't men and women sacrifice their lives for
the ideals of communism, socialism, and nationalism? I instinctively knew that these were not for me. But what about public
service, philanthropic work, teaching, or some other cause that
I had not investigated? Perhaps *there* I could find a burning commitment to radiate my life.

In my early years I was not bothered with what was giving
me unease now. I wasn't looking for anything beyond escaping from Russia, and later, beyond getting an education and
a job. But now, having attained success, I was driven to find a
challenge beyond it. My search in the various religions drew me
closer to their wisdoms, but it was more intellectual suste-
nance for the mind than substance for the heart.

As I began looking for some heart-embracing secular ideal,

a potential one came across my desk in the form of a book I received from one of my Moral Re-Armament friends entitled *Small Is Beautiful*, by E. F. Schumacher, a renowned English economist. I was enthralled by his views, first because they confirmed mine, and second, because he articulated them much more convincingly. Business giantism, he claimed, leads to alienation, bureaucracy, centralization, and ultimately to character erosion. But neither did he suggest going back to the ox and the plow. He favored using moderate instead of ultra-advanced technology, keeping commerce on the human scale with millions of small businesses instead of a few big ones. Looking down from a hundred-story building and seeing people and autos crawling like ants is not progress. Nor is robotism that robs people of work. People should not be driven by economics; economics should be harnessed to people's happiness.

Schumacher's economic credo gave impetus to my business philosophy but was not striking enough to equal the challenge I was looking for.

small   small   small   small   small

I HAD FEW ENCOURAGEMENTS for my quest and many doubts. My friends and associates wouldn't have given a second thought to what I was looking for. If it had been some secondary goal, I might have given up, but because I felt its ultimate importance, I stayed the course.

Because I was on the lookout for ideas, a brochure from The Aspen Institute of Humanistic Studies attracted my attention. It described a two-week retreat among the beautiful Colorado mountains for twenty businessmen to discuss directions for their lives. It was an irresistible invitation. Some of the moderators who attended the two-week seminars that were held throughout the summer were: Justice William Brennan of the U.S. Supreme Court, Dr. Karl Menninger of the Menninger Clinic, Dr. Albert Schweitzer, labor-leader William Reuther, philosopher Mortimer Adler, and other internationally renowned personages.

I signed up, and as preparation for the discussions, they suggested selected readings from Plato, the Bible, Karl Marx, Gunnar Myrdal, and others—seminal ideas that covered the intellectual spectrum of our civilization. I was the only small businessman among the academic moderators and corporate executives.

After two weeks of brilliant discussions, I came away with more knowledge about the sweep of civilization's institutions, but more important, with a dawning realization that there was a difference between intellectual and spiritual human nature. I compared the Aspen participants with the men and women I had met at Moral Re-Armament. Both were of the thinking elite, but the MRA people had an extra dimension—warm hearts in addition to reasoning minds. The Aspen group was more interested in how world institutions molded human nature, while the MRA people focused on how human nature shaped institutions. They insisted that you can't make a good omelet out of bad eggs—that is, no matter how well a religious, political, or social institution is organized, if the stock of people supporting it act on the basis of their lower human nature, the organization will reflect their defects. However, even if an institution is not well conceived, but its people are reaching to express their higher human nature, it will be more beneficial to more people than the other way around.

I came away from the Aspen experience with a lot of valuable information about various civilizations, but I was not smitten with any idea on which I could center my life.

± ∓ ± ∓ ± ∓

BECAUSE MY DESIRE to find the quintessential beyond success was as great as my desire to become Americanized, I persevered despite my mounting doubts.

On a visit to San Francisco, I heard Norman Cousins, then editor of *The Saturday Review of Literature*, give an impassioned speech for the need of world government. The time has come, he said, that just as one person cannot impose his or her will on another, so one nation should not have the right to impose its will on another nation. By giving up sovereignty to declare war and by relying on international world law, nations would take a giant step toward eliminating the scourge of war. His talk sounded much like the minister's sermon I had heard years earlier when I attended a Unitarian service.

But this time the idea gripped my imagination. When I came home, I studied it in some depth and joined the local chapter of the United World Federalists. When I gave several talks to local groups, I was ridiculed.

"Why should we give up sovereignty to a bunch of countries that don't share our values?"

Undaunted, I kept up my interest and was appointed to the Midwest Board of the U.W.F. and attended one of their conferences in Kansas city. As at the Aspen seminar, the discussions were brilliant, but not inspiring.

I noted a telling contrast between the U.W.F. institution-builders and the MRA human-nature changers. While the intellectual discussions about strengthening the United Nations were going on, there were distracting rumors that the leader of the conference and one of the delegates had become lovers and were planning to divorce their spouses. It reminded me of the Aspen seminar, where a corporation president was found in bed with one of the participants' wives.

I compared these incidents with the behavior of people in the dozen MRA conferences I attended, where I had not encountered a single indiscretion. As I meditated on my explorations for what lay beyond success, I felt that the contrasts between MRA and U.W.F. were getting me closer to what I was looking for. I was learning the critical difference between morality and intellectuality.

UWF   UWF   UWF   UWF

DURING ONE OF MY QUIET TIMES, I was hit with the disturbing thought that I was concentrating too much on my quest, and on myself, and not enough on helping people. My four-pronged theory of Meditation, Evaluation, Transformation, and Implementation led me directly to a practical idea. I would ease off from looking beyond success and concentrate on writing a book on how to help young people become successful in the real-estate business. My teaching helped a few, and the book might help thousands.

I spent hundreds of hours writing and rewriting before Prentice-Hall agreed to publish my book under the title *How to Use Leverage to Make Money in Local Real Estate*. I poured all I knew into it, citing in chapter-and-verse fashion what works and what doesn't. It sold 100,000 copies. I received dozens of letters from many parts of the country thanking me for the helpful information. Some telephoned, others wrote asking for more explanations.

An attorney called from Pittsburgh with the following problem:

"I own a building with a single tenant—a bank. Its $25,000-a-year lease is expiring and the bank wants to buy my property for $250,000 and spend another $500,000 to modernize it. I've depreciated the building to zero, and if I sell it, I won't have much more than $150,000 after taxes. If I invest it in a savings and loan at, say, 6 percent, my income will shrink to $9,000 a year. Got some idea how I can do better than that?"

I gave it a few moments' thought and then an idea struck me.

"Tell the bank president," I said, slowly gathering my thoughts, "that *you'll* spend $500,000 to upgrade your building and then lease it to him for 30 years."

"But I don't have the money."

"Borrow it."

"From whom?"

"From the bank—your present lessee. Get a $500,000 mortgage at 7 percent—a point higher than the current interest rate—on a 30-year amortization, so the loan terminates at the same time as the bank's 30-year lease. Then net lease the remodeled building to the bank based on a value of $750,000, with a return rate of 10 percent, or $75,000 a year. Now listen carefully. Since your payments on the $500,000, 30-year mortgage will be about $40,000 a year, you'll be left with a cash flow of $35,000 a year. That's a lot better than selling it and being left with $9,000 a year."

"I'm beginning to get what you're driving at," the attorney said, "and I want to thank you for a wonderful suggestion. But I can see the bank president saying to me, 'You want to borrow $500,000 at 7 percent, yet you want $75,000 rent based on a 10 percent return.' How do I counter that?"

I thought for a while and tried this idea for a starter:

"How old are you?"

"Fifty-five."

"You'll be 85 when this $35,000 annuity ends. Why don't you sweeten the deal by agreeing to convey the property to the bank for one dollar at the end of 30 years."

"That's not a bad idea either, because I won't be needing much at 85—if I live that long."

"Your heirs may not like this plan, but my concern is to get you the most spendable money during your lifetime. This, in my estimation, does it. You can refine it, but don't change the basic idea."

"You've given me lots to think about and I'm grateful."

"And I'm grateful to *you* for furnishing me an interesting item for my next book. You see, your problem will benefit others."

"Well, thanks again." And he hung up.

A half-year later, I received a letter that the bank had accepted the plan with few modifications.

% $ % $ % $

MY EXPERIENCES IN SEEKING what lies beyond success were beginning to have an indirect effect on my thinking. My reflective moods led me to self-exploration. Why did I experience a sense of *serenity* when I was *giving*, and *intensity* when I was *getting*? That led me to becoming aware of the measurable difference between, on the one hand, giving and expecting a return, and, on the other, giving *without* expecting a reward. No matter how good my feeling was of satisfying someone, it was always tainted with *getting* something in return—goodwill, a favor, a future reward, etc. I noticed that when I gave without expecting a return, the feeling sparked inspiration.

Spurred on by these ruminations, I got involved in an adventure of giving that tested my musings in a practical way.

Two hundred large families with scant means were living on welfare in rat-infested basements. There was a housing crisis for these poor families, and the public media made it visible with pathetic pictures and heart-rending stories.

The city owned vacant lots of razed properties that could be bought for a nominal amount, and the federal government under Title 35 offered 100-percent financing to families who qualified as underprivileged. I joined the two facts into a plan of action that the *Milwaukee Journal* prominently featured in a lengthy news story.

I suggested that wealthy individuals or corporations buy the unsightly, weed-filled lots from the city and build low-cost four-bedroom homes, which upon completion would be conveyed to poor families. I concluded the description of my plan with an offer to build twenty of those houses myself.

The story stirred up a great deal of interest, and I was invited to appear on television with an activist priest who had gained national attention in connection with a militant group of protesters known as the Black Panthers. Several black leaders who were also on the program spoke in favor of my idea, but the white priest lashed out at me.

"You slippery real-estate guys are all alike. You're only interested in feathering your own nests. If we dug deep enough into Bockl's plan, we'd find some trick—more interested in himself than in the poor."

I was stunned. This coming from a priest whom I admired because of his good work in the black community! I reacted impulsively and unthinkingly.

"What makes you think," I asked, "that you and your Black Panthers have a monopoly on doing good?"

One of the Black Panthers in the priest's entourage rushed to the speaker's table, shaking his fist at me and shouting, "You'll get this in your face if you talk like that to our Father!"

A black leader sitting next to me probably saved me from being assaulted on live television when he raised his hand and said, "Okay, Tom, let Mr. Bockl continue; maybe something good will come out of this."

The confrontation toned me down, but not enough to prevent me from pursuing my main objective as I beamed my words to the TV audience.

"My plan, as I've described it, is practical and can take many of these large families out of their miserable basements if corporations and individuals will respond. Let's not be swayed by the negative attitude expressed here tonight. Let's *do* what's right rather than haggle about *who's* right. And to put action where my mouth is, I'm going on record publicly tonight, as I did in the *Milwaukee Journal*, that I will build twenty four-bedroom houses for twenty large, needy families."

"He'll never do it; and if he does, it'll be because there'll be a big profit for him!" a Black Panther ranted with raised fist from the back of the room.

I hired a young man with a Master's degree in real estate and instructed him to buy twenty vacant lots, familiarize himself with the FHA rules of Title 35, hire an architect to draw plans, get contract bids, and visit social agencies to help select the poor families who were most desperately in need of housing.

After eighteen months of pioneering work, this man, under my close supervision, conveyed twenty brand-new, four-bedroom houses to twenty needy families with six or more children. The county welfare department, of course, made the mortgage payments on the properties, but the families owned them. Because there was no profit to anyone and because of the low interest on the mortgages, the payments were only slightly higher than what the county was already paying for them in rent. My helper and I arranged to have a social worker aid the families in maintaining and caring for the homes.

My contribution to this project was the $15,000 I paid to the young man plus my effort in guiding it through completion. The glowing feeling I experienced when I visited the large families in their new homes and saw the happy looks in their eyes was of a higher nature than that of successful real-estate venturing.

FIRED UP WITH THE CONCEPT of giving without a return, I immediately began looking for another pro-bono project. I didn't have long to look, because *it* found *me*.

A young couple with degrees in sociology and psychology obtained some federal seed-money to care for several retarded infants between the ages of one and five. They were children of husbandless mothers who didn't know how to care for these infants. A friend of mine, a professor of sociology, had become the couple's advisor.

"George," he said at lunch one day, "I need your help. There's a tremendous unmet need among infants who are wasting away at their homes because their mothers aren't capable of caring for them. Jon and Barbara, two former students of mine, have made a start toward solving this acute problem. They are presently in a dilapidated basement caring for a few infants, but there are many more who need their help. To do a professional job, they need a modest school for fifty infants and twenty-five teachers. I've done some checking. To build a new school would cost a million dollars. There's no public money available for such a school. But I've organized a board of directors with a few socialites who might be able to raise $350,000 from private donations for a Montessori project."

"Where do *I* come in?"

"I'm putting you on the board to find an old building that will lend itself to recycling into a school for fifty children at a cost of no more than $350,000. You're an expert at it. There's no greater need I know of to which you can put your remodeling expertise than to help these hapless infants and their helpless mothers."

The eloquent plea had a double challenge—to help the helpless and to test my recycling skill in building a million-dollar facility for $350,000.

I explored a dozen buildings and ruled them out either because of price, location, or inadequate structure. Eventually, my search led to a vacated 20,000-square-foot bowling-alley building that was owned by a Savings and Loan Association on a $500,000 foreclosure. For years the sturdy structure had been gathering dust and taxes, adding loss upon loss. I bought it for the Montessori School for $105,000 with $15,000 down.

The socialites went to work raising the $350,000 while I collaborated with an architect and contractors to fit the school's needs into our limited budget. My conviction that deep inside the heart of man is a yearning to do good was amply illustrated by the dozen subcontractors who cut their profits—or eliminated them—in order to make their contribution to the worthy project. A year later the money was raised, the school was built, and the facilities were as complete and modern as they were originally planned to be in the new million-dollar building.

At the dedication, my professor friend ended his remarks with:

"All of you who participated in this noble work will experience a healing therapy, different only in kind from the healing the infants will receive in this beautiful school that volunteerism built."

Today, eighteen years later, the school has tripled in size with a multi-million-dollar annual budget, caring for hundreds of needy infants from the mushrooming growth of teenage pregnancies.

WITH MY QUEST for what's beyond success on hold, and with two rewarding pro-bono ventures behind me, I turned once more to innovative real-estate venturing—but now, more than before, with a contributive dimension. To prepare for it, I made two bold moves. I gave up my residential brokerage business and sold my income-producing properties because my focus was now more on creating new projects than on collecting rents. To save my salesmen's jobs, I transferred my real-estate brokerage department to one of my former salesmen who owned a flourishing realty company. It turned out to be a good business strategy as well. Many of my competitors, who favored holding on to their real estate, were caught in cyclical economic downturns and lost their holdings for lack of liquidity. By selling some of my properties, I was in a good cash position to risk new pioneering ventures, which fulfilled me more than owning and managing properties.

I picked a project that was as risky as it was innovative. A ten-story, 150,000-square-foot building in the heart of Milwaukee's downtown was offered for sale by a furniture-store owner who was going out of business. After eyeing it for several purposes, I bought it with the intention of converting it into a use that, as far as I knew, had never been attempted in America. I would recycle the dust-laden furniture warehouse into a 110 shops-in-apartments—that is, each apartment was to have a store or service business in front and living quarters in the back—a sort of nostalgic return to fifty years ago, when the proprietor of a corner store lived in a few rooms behind his business establishment. The more I thought about the idea, the more I liked it. I knew it would be difficult to finance and rent the unorthodox shop-in-apartment concept, but that only whetted my appetite.

I pictured 110 storekeepers selling plants, gourmet foods, unusual glassware, art—or operating a beauty salon, a photograph studio, or a small-appliance repair shop—all combining their business with their living quarters.

As I suspected would be the case, I was turned down by several Savings and Loan Associations because of the untried, mixed use. But at just about that time, city officials became interested in developing downtown residential apartments. With their help, I got the Housing and Urban Development Agency (HUD) to take a look at my unorthodox plan. They agreed to a $3 million loan, provided I abandoned the shop-in-apartment idea and rented exclusively to residential tenants. I refused. I was primarily interested in pioneering the mixed-use idea.

After months of negotiating, we struck a compromise. If I couldn't rent the 110 units on the basis of shops-in-apartments within a year, I would agree to lease the apartments left vacant as residences. In return, HUD agreed to bend their rules by allowing me to preserve the old-world charm of the twelve-foot loft ceiling (their manual called for eight-foot ceilings), to expose the concrete columns and ceiling beams (their rules required they be covered), and to eliminate all partitions within apartments except for washrooms (their regulations specified room divisions)—because, I contended, downtown rental units would interest only couples or singles who didn't need partitions.

Because HUD was interested in creating downtown apartments, they went out on a limb with me. We differed because they were as concerned about their underwriting judgment as I was about tenant acceptance of my unusual project.

After mailing 5000 beautiful brochures, doing extensive advertising, and getting several pictured feature articles in newspapers, I was able to lease only thirty apartments my way and was obliged to lease the rest HUD's way. Milwaukee simply didn't have 110 unusual people to try an unusual idea in an unusual building. But the thirty tenants were delighted to combine their living-quarters with a health spa, beauty salon, photograph studio, flower shop, hearing-aid shop, and other sundry services.

It was a partial success, but the tenants, with the mix and without, enjoyed the So-Ho loft look of their apartments. They had fun partitioning their open spaces with Chinese silk, shutters, and other ways that gave them a sense of excitement in expressing their individual tastes. Some designs were artistically outstanding.

Fourteen years later, *The Chalet at the River*, as it's called, is one of my and HUD's outstanding projects. After all expenses and debt service, it nets $200,000 a year.

MY NEXT REAL-ESTATE VENTURE dealt as much with changing people as with changing the use of a building.

Thirty years ago, what were the hippies trying to tell us? I talked to many of them and thoughtfully tried to sift through their complaints.

Many were aimless protesters, but a thinking minority made sense. They found the Establishment cold and callous, driving to succeed without slowing down to help them.

I bought a vacant 40,000-square-foot auto-agency building for conversion into a mini-mall of small shops that lent themselves to giving hippies a chance for a piece of the action—to change protesters into entrepreneurs.

Twenty thousand people lived within a two-mile radius of the former auto agency. Here, I figured, was the purchasing power necessary for local small business to thrive. This type of recycling had never been done before, and that's why it triggered my interest.

With pioneering optimism, I leased stores to hippies who I knew were financially weak, but with the expectancy that they would grow entrepreneurial muscles. I leased 1000 square feet to a young couple who had been operating a run-down record store under the name of Dirty Jack's Record Shop. They promised to clean up their name to Jack's Record Shop. Within a year, I leased the entire mall to twenty-three merchants, most of them first-time proprietors. The eager young tenants, dressed in "Establishment" clothes, were selling plants, purses, yogurt, art, greeting cards, candy, clothes, antiques, books, ethnic foods, jewelry, and a variety of gift items.

The hippies soon discovered that it was easier to protest than to stay in the black! They were developing a new respect for the Establishment.

A third of the tenants became rent-delinquent after three months. Lack of experience, goofing off, and insufficient capital were the reasons.

Failure breeds meanness. I was accused of poor management, and the young tenants, who had joyfully applauded my efforts when they signed their leases, now tore them up and left. My rent roll dropped from $15,000 to $10,000 a month. The project was in the red.

I wrestled with the mall's plight in my quiet time. My good intentions were dashed—but *were* they? I listened:

Didn't I know that several of Milwaukee's large shopping centers had a two-to-three year shake-out before they became successful? And while several hippies left with rancorous feelings, didn't others prosper? A young couple selling art prints, Jack's Record Shop, two young women operating a tiny print shop, a black woman selling men's accessories—all made it, and all were happily experiencing their first pride of entrepreneurship. Wasn't I making a contribution in helping beginners get started? What if I *was* losing $2,000 a month? Doesn't pioneering entail some sacrifice? Doesn't financial defeat teach a kind of wisdom that financial success does not?

After several years of financial sputtering, the Prospect Mall became a beehive of activity as stronger tenants who replaced the weak ones carved small, new niches into the Establishment. It was not one of my successes, but the good feeling of changing protesters into entrepreneurs compensated for its mediocre financial showing.

7

CROSSING THE FRONTIER INTO THE PATHLESS UNKNOWN

*It's Possible to Have a Quiet Time, Where You Can
Have an Inaudible Conversation with God.*

DURING A BUSINESS LULL, MY UNFINISHED quest for what lay beyond success surged once again! After my extensive religious and secular investigations, I decided the time had come to formulate my own concept of God, and God's relationship to humankind, based on what I had learned from thousands of hours of reading sublime literature and from hundreds of theological and secular discussions with knowledgeable men and women. I found that it was much easier to read and discuss than to create a universal spiritual credo to fulfill me, just as denominational beliefs fulfill sectarians.

My starting point was that the most renowned scientists and seers don't know how and why the universe came into being. What we do know is that it exists and functions according to a Cosmic Intelligence based on laws, the foremost of which is the law of evolution.

From there I took my conjecturing on a course that involved the wisdoms of the East and West, but modified by my subjective interpretations.

My first major departure from Western thinking was to bring

God down from heaven to earth, from a vague abstraction to a Spark of God operating within my mind and body.

To help my picturization of God, I accepted the East's conjecturing that God is a Cosmic Energy distributed throughout the universe to keep its myriad parts functioning—from galaxies to the nucleus of the atom. From that precept I deduced that a Cosmic Spark, or a Spark of God, is the actual God within me, directing the functioning of my mind and body, and that my individualized consciousness is an extension of its creative process.

In the West, that Spark is referred to as the Soul; in the East, it is the Monad, or Permanent Atom. Because of modern technology, I take this concept a step further. With the advent of microchips, I add a synonym to Soul or Monad—a live genetic chip that records information from experience, thus bringing whatever propensities are developed in this incarnation to the next. That's how people inherit the good and the bad of previous incarnations—and are born with the printouts of the past.

With this as a backdrop, I convinced myself that the Spark of God within me was the same as the God of the sacred scriptures—except, instead of being somewhere "out there" in heaven, God was as near to me as my next breath. In other words, there is not creation *and* God, but Creation *is* God.

Because I wanted my God to be more vital and practical than the One I left, I evolved a plan to test myself whether I was actively guided from where I was to where I wanted to go. To measure the change, I used the standard of what's pro-life and what's anti-life. I had no problem drawing the distinction in a general way: Jesus' profound, pro-life truth of turning the other cheek, and the Buddha's anti-life truth that intense desire is the cause of humankind's miseries.

However, distinguishing the subtle nuances between pro-life and anti-life on a personal, specific basis is where God's nature and human nature clash. To help solve this, I've conceived what I call a dialogue with God. When a blurring problem of what's right and wrong comes up, I take it to my quiet time and evaluate it. If it's ennobling, it's *God* expressing *pro-life*; if it's negative, it's *me* leaning toward *anti-life*. I call this reasoning process a dialogue with God because I can't reason with my own consciousness. Then with whom else is it I'm dialoguing if not the Life Force that's sustaining me? I'm not off the mark to conclude that my questioning thoughts are answered by the Spark of God that guides me. The fact that our conversation is inaudible does not mean it's not taking place. The most powerful and wise evolutionary forces in nature are invisible and inaudible.

Having a dialogue with God makes more demands on me than my occasional synagogue attendance did. It's a clarifier of right from wrong.

A few mundane examples:

A contractor diverted $30,000 of a plumbing bill on a home I was building to my *Chalet at the River* project.

"This'll save you $10,000 of income taxes," he said.

"No, Bob. Bill it to my home."

"Okay; I just wanted to do you a favor."

It was anti-law, therefore anti-life. Dialoguing with God turned doubt opposed to saving $10,000 into certainty.

I have no problem with the infidelities swirling around me. I measure unfaithfulness by its anti-life consequences—the diminishing of myself, my wife, the third party, and the anti-moral effects on my children and society.

I neutralize slurs, sarcasm, false accusations, etc., with a pro-life approach of finding a way of elevating the offender instead of returning anti-life disparagements that spread the initial disturbance like a rock thrown in still waters. My meditative dialogues help me to do this if not most, then some of the time.

I try not to be impulsive and thoughtlessly compare people, because someone is thus diminished and that's anti-life.

Competing in the marketplace sometimes makes me squirm with indecision. Although I don't use anti-life tactics, I some-

times have to use competitiveness to win. I mitigate it somewhat by pioneering in ventures where there's little or no
competition.

I have no problem with putting the following into anti-life
categories: hunting, caging animals in zoos, forcing animals to
perform at circuses, and inflicting unnecessary cruelties on
animals in the name of scientific progress. I know there are pro-
life counterarguments to each of these; but in my estimation,
my positions are more in harmony with benevolent nature.

This pro-life/anti-life dialogue with God to measure my
spiritual discipline may sound like a lot of pap to theologians,
fundamentalists, or mainstream religionists; but for me, merely
being a "nice guy" within or outside a religion, though lauda-
tory, is not demanding enough to change my lower to a higher
human nature.

When my friend Gene Posner—astute lawyer, businessman, and millionaire—asked me to explain my concept of
God and how I used pro-life and anti-life to determine what's
right and wrong, his cool comment, after he listened politely,
was, "All you're doing is using good psychological sense. I don't
see any God connection."

"I know it's good sense, but what's the source? You say it
comes from 'I don't know' and 'I don't care.' I say it comes from
my God Spark that sustains my body and illumines my mind
with thoughts that lead to creativity. You've substituted mere
ethical humanism for the awe of God."

"As you know, I'm very practical. . . ."

"So am I. That's why I look for what's beyond success."

"I buy *success*, but not what's beyond it."

In the years that followed I continued to communicate with
God in my unorthodox way and jotted down thoughts that
came to me during quiet times. After sifting and winnowing the
best out of some 1000 entries, I published two books titled,
How to Find Something Big to Live For (with the subtitle
A Spiritual Odyssey) and *God Beyond Religion* (with the subtitle *Personal Journeyings from Religiosity to Spirituality*). Only

3000 copies were sold, compared to my four published real-estate books, which sold 300,000 copies. Obviously, *success* sells better than what's *beyond* success.

!　　!　　!　　!　　!　　!　　!

My concept that the Spark of God within me is more real than the anthropomorphic God I had known has not only helped my secular and spiritual progress, it has also guided me to some aspects of physical healing. When, for whatever reason, I'm beset with a headache, a squeamish stomach, a back problem, or other minor ailment, I don't rush for an aspirin or a doctor. I retire to a quiet corner of the house and put these thoughts in the pipeline of my mind:

I'm not going to let fear . . . anxiety . . . stress . . . control me. I'm going to relax and rely on the wisdom of my body to heal me—that pro-life force that draws its healing energy from the Universal Cosmic Energy to which it's linked. To the extent I'm convinced of this connection, to that extent will I receive its healing.

I've overcome dozens of minor ailments by letting such thoughts course through my mind. I don't pretend to be a healer, but for me it works! Some may regard this as playing games with God. I can understand their attitude, because I was there. But after years of searching for a Power beyond my own, after knocking on many doors for answers, I now know that having a personal dialogue with God is not an illusion, but a practical spiritual experience.

The experimenting with, and experiencing of, my concept of God without intermediaries keeps me out of the religious mainstream, but I have no problem relating to it. The inspirational insights I receive during my quiet times imbue me with a spirit of reasonableness and magnanimity so that I understand why there are religious fundamentalists, cultists, and atheists. Their views interest me but don't persuade me. I'm grateful that I live in a country where I can discuss my differences and retain the freedom to be different.

I find it exciting to be on the frontier between the known and the Unknown. My active dialogue with God clears murky perspectives, changes false values, provides new insights, and buttresses the rationale for a self-disciplined morality.

Quiet time taught me that quiet joy is longer lasting than the fireworks of raucous merriment that flashes brilliantly one moment and is extinguished the next. When I attended regional and national real-estate conventions, I had no problem separating myself from the loud, liquored talk and carousing that are always a part of convention conviviality. I don't condemn their frivolity, and I do enjoy matching their levity and humor with mine. But I'm "one of the boys" only up to a point. I prefer *my* kind of excitement—plunging into a prudent kind of incautious activity rather than reclining in cautious inactivity. My verve and audacity opened the radiant view that life is a constant adventurous becoming, a never-ending journey flashing with the grandeur of boundless vistas, evolving—incarnation after incarnation—in new and challenging times and environments. I like the idea of climbing and never arriving, where the exhilarating evolutionary journey itself becomes the destiny.

MY SEARCH TO LINK with the Unknown didn't prevent me from striking a balance between my spiritual probing and looking for unusual real-estate ventures.

This time I found one that surpassed all my previous undertakings—in originality, pro-bono fallout, and profitability—a win-win-win combination.

I read in several books and articles that 80 percent of new jobs are created by small businesses. In support of this, I heard a nationally renowned economist predict that the new informational age will spawn a cottage-type industry where the big corporations will farm out work to hundreds of thousands of small contractors, or specialists, who will produce in homes or low-cost office space.

This gave me an idea. I bought two sturdy old buildings and linked them to a plan of creating workspaces for small, white-collar factories—at rents so low that the small-business specialists could afford to take their work out of their homes and into my buildings.

Economic factors were in my favor. I bought the buildings, consisting of 200,000 square feet, for $4.00 a square foot. They were located in the historic Third Ward, an area that was economically asleep for fifty years. The owners were eager to get rid of them because they were vacant and losing money. I hired three small contractors to do the work—a retired electrician, a carpenter with two helpers, and a plumber who operated from his home. They were my basic remodeling team. With their economies, I was able to offer office space for as low as $4.00 a square foot, a fourth of what they would have to pay for comparable offices. The rationale of my plan was to build a large incubator-center for small new entrepreneurs. It also involved a large risk, because it had never been done before.

It took five years and $5 million to recycle and fill both buildings with 100 small entrepreneurs. It is the largest incubator for neophyte businesspersons in Wisconsin.

Seeing young men and women enthusiastically carve economic niches into my buildings was a uniquely rewarding experience. I got a vicarious kick out of seeing their businesses grow and felt gratified that I had played a role in it.

The eager enterprisers were as interesting as their small white-collar factories. A 25-year-old artist who was floundering aimlessly got an idea for building greeting-card stands out of plastic material. He leased 500 square feet in the basement to get started. Within six months he expanded to 2000 square feet. A national company that sold $50 million of greeting cards a year liked his design and contracted to replace all their wooden and wire stands with his plastic ones. Two years later my floundering hippie turned into a yuppie. He bought a 20,000-square-foot building and is now employing thirty full-time workers.

A 28-year-old man came to my office and confidently proclaimed that he was the best custom-furniture designer in Milwaukee. He asked if I would build a showroom on the first floor and a small workplace for him in the basement of my building. After checking with several people for whom he had built furniture and receiving favorable comments, I spent $25,000 for a penniless young man to get started.

He, his brother, and a helper moved into my space with a visible sense of joyous abandon. Their first customers were tenants in my building for whom they built strikingly unusual desks at half the cost of similar business furniture. They filled their showroom with samples of their craft: out-of-the-ordinary beds, sofas, and armoires.

The piece that caught my eye was a cocktail table with a surface of ninety-nine moveable cubes, each of the six sides with a different lacquered color. Thus the table could be arranged to show all yellow, green, blue, red, white, black, or any combination of the six colors. It was priced at $1,000 and sold as soon as it was displayed.

A year later he got an order from a New York corporation executive to build twenty-five pieces of furniture for his multi-million-dollar home. And two years later he asked me to let him out of his lease because his space had become too small for his growing business. I released him and rerented it to a photo lab. He moved into his own 10,000-square-foot building. My penniless hippie, like the greeting-card-stand artist, had also become a yuppie.

A specialist in preparing machinery manuals left his job and formed his own company with one helper in a tiny office in my building. Three years later, he had expanded into 6000 square feet with a workforce of twenty people. They wrote operating manuals for Toyota and some of the largest corporations in America.

Most of the new, white-collar entrepreneurs were young men and women who built their small enterprises around some specialized knowledge. Matre specialized in designing products for large manufacturers. Enlargement Works, a man-and-wife team with expertise in enlarging small prints into artistic blowups, grew from 800 to 5000 square feet, and from two to ten workers. K and S, a photo lab starting with three people, has expanded into 9000 square feet, is using a half-million dollars' worth of equipment, and is providing work for forty employees. Peterson Consulting, Ltd. furnishes computerized legal information to help lawyers prepare their briefs for trials. Spectrum has a 15-foot-high ceiling where it shoots videos for television ads. Visuals Plus creates computer graphics and programs for accounting and marketing departments of large corporations. And Hintz Associates, a public-relations firm, began operations in a bedroom at home and grew in my building from 500 to 3500 square feet.

Of approximately 100 small businesses that moved into my buildings, about ten failed and ninety prospered. My master plan to create commercial space at low prices for small white-collar factories was a huge success. Because I bought the old buildings at low prices and used a team of small contractors to recycle them, my cash flow profit after all expenses and debt service is an astounding $400,000 a year. But in addition to the dazzling bottom line, I revived two dying buildings, gave new life to an old neglected neighborhood, created $5 million worth of work, gave birth to 100 new entrepreneurs, and originated 500 new jobs.

𐀀   𐀀   𐀀   𐀀   𐀀   𐀀

THE SWIRLING SOCIAL and economic events interested me, and whatever time I could wrest from my meditative and business commitments I used for making a minuscule dent in ongoing affairs. Running for public office didn't appeal to me, nor did I think I would be good at it. I decided to make what difference I could by publishing about fifty essays over a period of fifteen years that reached the 600,000 readers of the *Milwaukee Journal*'s Op-Ed Page. They ranged over a variety of subjects, always emphasizing the good and enduring, in contrast to the news stories about fraud, sex, and crime. Here are the titles of a number of them, which fairly described their contents: .

God Is a Reach, Not a Crutch

Why the Pious Are Bias

When Desire Is on Fire—Beware

The Law of Karma Works Unerringly

Reincarnation—Fact or Fancy?

A Pitch for Old-Fashioned Love and Marriage

When the Family Crumbles, Civilization Crumbles

The Arabs and Jews Should Share Palestine the Way Germans, French, and Italians Share Switzerland

Spirituality Is More Therapeutic than Psychiatry

The Survival of the Wisest Is More Relevant Today than the Survival of the Fittest

It's More Important to Change Human Nature than Institutions

Because I was a businessman rather than a theologian or clergyman, writing on these subjects raised inquisitive eyebrows. Why would a busy real-estate developer fool around with such nonbusiness ideas? Of all the favorable, often negative, and even puzzling reactions, I prize the one from the religious editor of the *Journal*, James Johnson, who wrote:

"With your unifying spiritual thinking, you've articulated a moral tone for our community which, because it comes from a businessman rather than a clergyman, attracted more attention and therefore provoked new thinking."

I gave a lot of thought to the differences between what is smart, what is intelligent, what is wise, and what is spiritual. They interested me because I believed that discussing their contrasts went a long way toward blueprinting and building values to live by.

Being smart is one-dimensional, inherited from our lower human nature when we used it cunningly during the cave era to fight animals, later on the battlefield, and now in social and business relationships. I've seen smart tycoons and con men reveal their one-dimensional vestiges in their tense faces, shifty body-language, and fast talk. They're smart in getting out of tight corners, but not intelligent enough to see that they're short-changing their lives with quick, one-dimensional victories.

Intelligence is two-dimensional, having evolved from the cunning and aggressive to the reasonable and intellectual. It has produced the scholars, professionals, business executives, clergy, politicians, and the general workforce in a country's infrastructure. They make less money than the "street smart," but they don't stoop to their scrounging level.

Abel Berland, one of the most intelligent men I know and a dear friend, was president of the Arthur Rubloff Co. During one of their business discussions, Rubloff said: "Abel, you're intelligent, but I'm smart. That's why you work for me, not I for you." Rubloff was smart all right, but not intelligent to know the difference between one- and two-dimensional living.

I've mingled with the intelligent at Aspen Institute seminars, United World Federalist meetings, Religion and International Affairs conclaves, and at other cerebral conferences. They're interesting and attractive people, but without wisdom to soften their intellect, many turn knowledge into a god and become information experts.

Intelligent painters, writers, musicians, and actors who win fame for their work often become pathological drunkards and debauchees—an incongrious mix of trying to elevate society and debasing themselves. Perhaps Nikos Kazantzakis, the world-famous Greek writer, had the answer to the plight of the unwise intelligent. Wallowing in the existential trough of Sartre and Camus, wavering between despair, intellectualism, and detachment, Kazantzakis finally fulfilled his life when he accepted the reality of spiritual wisdom. There, he said, he found peace and serenity.

Wisdom is three-dimensional. It's an evolutionary leap from intelligence, a comprehensive insight beyond the intellect. I saw it in action. The wise opine less and observe more. They're seldom in a hurry. They're confident without arrogance, generous without reservation, vulnerable without fear, and graceful without trying.

The wise combine wisdom and intelligence to ennoble their good works. I know of a brilliant attorney who took a public-defender job at one-fifth the salary he could have earned in a prestigious law firm; a physician who is healing the starving in Ethiopia instead of living a luxurious life in America; and a young executive who gave up his $150,000-a-year job supervising nursing homes to care for an orphanage at a fraction of his salary.

These wise men are poised for an active linkage with God in the spiritual realm, the fourth dimension.

I read a book on the *mathematical* fourth dimension, and because I'm a right-brainer, I couldn't understand or enjoy probing it. For me it's far more stimulating to probe the spiritual, where there's more purpose-revealing, life-sustaining fruitage than in mathematical materialism.

Spirituality is a nondenominational yearning for linkage with God. However, I'm fully aware that religiosity has elevated the human natures of hundreds of millions of people, and though it divided them, the good far outweighed the bad.

My illiterate mother, for instance, derived her caring nature from what the rabbi told her about Judaism's biblical God. The Torah was the rock upon which she built her life. Had I attempted to explain away her God and substituted mine, I would have pulled the rock from under her and left her in utter confusion and despair. It would have been as impossible to change her beliefs as it is impossible to uncondition today's hundreds of millions from their faiths.

Then why have I chosen to replace religiosity with spirituality? Because I want to be in the forefront of religious evolution, in the company of those who want God as ardently as the most devout fundamentalists, but without their dogmatic formulations. We want it pure, free, and direct, without meddling intermediaries. To back up my choice, I use my four prerequisites for change—Meditation, Evaluation, Transformation, and Implementation. The first two are relatively easy, but Transformation and Implementation are difficult. Erasing former conditioning and bucking religious peer-pressure are formidable obstacles. But I'm determined to persevere, because only when we make religious evolutionary progress shall we arrive at the coming of the next spiritual epoch. Hundreds of years from now, dogmatic religion will be as much a vestige of the past as heathenism is now.

As I continue probing the wonders of spirituality, I'll be making changes in my never-ending evolutionary journey. And I'll be enjoying it, because it's putting sizzle into the mix of balancing my secular and spiritual activity.

8

HOW THE SECULAR AND SPIRITUAL
REINFORCE EACH OTHER

*Life Is Never-Ending, Constantly Evolving
into Eternity; and the Evolutionary Journey
Is the Destiny.*

B ECAUSE I KNOW WHO I AM, HOW I'M EVOLV-
ing, and where I'm going, I'm not confused about my
identity, ethnicity, or religion. My spiritual search has
liberated me from these allegiances, and I'm enjoying my freedom in an enlightened country where pluralism and sepa-
ration of state and religion prevail. That's why I'm grateful for
my liberty and feel obliged and privileged to do all I can
for America's welfare.

I have no problem relating to, and participating wholeheartedly with, ethnics and religionists of all kinds who think dif-
ferently than I. And because I understand why they believe the
way they do, I'm as comfortable in their presence as they are
in mine.

Just as conceptualizing the four prerequisites of guts, imagination, persuasion, and integrity have guided me to real-estate
success, so the concept of Meditation, Evaluation, Transformation, and Implementation has helped my pioneering quest
to find the challenge beyond success. In practicing it, I try to
avoid quoting religious platitudes and becoming a nuisance. I've

therefore formulated a practical plan for actualizing my aspirations. It involves four specifics: Managing the *physical, emotional, mental,* and *spiritual* aspects of my life. Although they interrelate, each requires a focused approach.

A HEALTHY BODY REQUIRES a troika of disciplines: proper food, exercise, and rest. Good health doesn't happen serendipitously. Proper food is the alpha and omega of physical health. But because there are so many contradictory opinions from doctors, nutritionists, and food hucksters, it's easy to become confused.

I unconfused myself with the help of my wife, who read many reports about what's good and bad food. We attended a two-day seminar staffed by a panel of experts who specialized in food science. The keynote speaker was Harvey Diamond whose book *Fit for Life* sold a million copies. When I put it all together, I came to the conclusion that food is at its best when eaten raw, in its natural state, before it's contaminated with fat, salt, condiments, sugar, dairy products, and heat. I know it's a radical and controversial departure from all kinds of tantalizing gourmet dishes to junk-food concoctions, and all combinations in between. Then what's there left to eat?

The answer: an immense variety of uncooked fruits, vegetables, and nuts. The food scientists contended that our bodies are more like those of apes who eat fruits, nuts, and vegetables, and unlike carnivorous felines and milk-drinking calves. The unnatural foods—from fried junk to cooked gourmet—accumulate toxins in the body, overload the cells with sludge, and eventually break down the weakest organs in the body.

The food scientists contrasted a breakfast menu of juice from four freshly squeezed oranges and a half pineapple with one of fried eggs, ham, and a glass of milk. They contrasted a lunch of two ripe bananas, two peaches, a pear, and two ounces of pecan nuts with a noon meal of a hamburger, cheese, french fries, and coffee. And for supper they contrasted a bowl of cut tomatoes, avocados, cauliflower, broccoli, and two ounces of unsalted walnuts with a steak dinner of dead animal carcass, baked potatoes, and a slice of chocolate cake washed down with two cups of coffee. The food gurus summarized the contrasts in the three meals thus: One cleanses the body, the other pollutes; one provides energy without residue, the other provides less energy with more sludge.

The food scientists told the 300 people in the audience that we're on the threshold of a food revolution; that fifty years from now we'll have more fruitarian-vegetarians than carnivores; that just as we're now convinced that smoking damages lungs, so we'll become convinced that the present American diet overloads the body with toxic wastes that clog arteries and shorten lives.

I met their challenge to join the food revolution only partway. I accepted their suggested menus of fruit juice for breakfast and a bowl of fruit and nuts for lunch; but for supper I slip in some poached salmon occasionally with my plate of vegetables. During business luncheons, I limit myself to a bowl of soup, and when I take my family to a restaurant, I alternate between a vegetarian dinner and some kind of fish. At banquets or conferences, I eat the vegetables around the entree. My food discipline will not appeal to lovers of either gourmet or junk food, but, as in real-estate pioneering, I want to be on the cutting edge of the food revolution. As of now, my diet consists of 60 percent fruit, 20 percent vegetables, 5 percent nuts, and 15 percent non-ideal foods.

An essential "nutrient" for a sound body is exercise. Here, too, there are many contradictory opinions. After investigating a half dozen, I came to the conclusion that since I was not interested in pumping iron to build muscles, walking was the best exercise for me. Consequently, during the last thirty years

I've walked three miles every day, or once around the world. It's a staggering distance, and I'm sure that all my muscles and organs were the beneficiaries of its healing effects.

Walking three miles daily, especially in wooded areas, is my retreat, my holy time of the day. It's where I recharge my body and clear my mind of trivia. I look forward to it with the same eagerness as the clergy do to ceremonials, but mine is without distractions.

In addition to walking, I've played—with less than average ability—five years of touch football, ten years of league bowling, twenty years of tennis. These I then gave up for golf, which I still play from two to three times a week. When I break a hundred, I celebrate with drinking a glass of orange juice.

Rest is the other side of exercise. The benefits of an hour's walk are lost unless it's followed immediately with a half hour of rest. I discovered that when I plunge directly after a walk into conversation, business phoning, or eating, the afterglow fades and the serenity ends.

Another form of rest that I find indispensable is a twenty-minute lie-down before eating my evening meal. After an active day, a respite refreshes me for the evening. More relaxing than a martini, which deadens some and stimulates others, is cooperating with nature. The martini artificializes it.

Do my ideas on diet, exercise, and rest sound too much like regimentation? They shouldn't. They constitute a common-sense way of getting the rush out of living.

MANAGING MY EMOTIONS requires more wisdom than caring for my body, especially the problems of handling ambition, aggresion, and hostility. It poses the antinomy between the eye-for-an-eye approach and turning the other cheek—each a credible option. My concern is not how to deal with extreme violence or tyrants like Hitler or Stalin. That's another philosophical subject. My practical challenge is how to best solve the daily mundane problems that impinge on my emotions.

My search beyond success provided wiser answers than those I found in psychology. That's because mine are based on the Buddha's and Jesus' profound truths, which reach beyond the intellect. My challenge is how to make these truths come alive with action that's more spiritual than intellectual.

A few examples:

I abated the rent for a photographer amounting to $11,000 to help him overcome a cash-flow problem. At the end of the abatement, he moved out, breaking the balance of a two-year lease. My first impulse was anger because he conned me. My second, a day later, was to calm down and do nothing. Suing him would bring self-satisfaction, but also a hornet's nest of hostility which would emotionally engulf both of us. I dropped the matter. Doing nothing was not world-shaking wisdom, but it avoided a battering of my emotions.

My host/guest management philosophy took a hit from a tenant who sued me for $20,000 because he claimed he lost business as a result of poor management of my building. He studied the building code and called the building inspector to view what he drummed up as violations. When the inspector found none, he called city-council members and the mayor, and followed that up with bad-mouthing me to the 110 tenants in the building. He called me at home late at night offering to settle for several thousand dollars. I refused.

I was wavering between teaching him a lesson for his obvious mischief and settling (and forgetting) it. I called him to my office.

"Henry, you're smart, but not intelligent. You could be earning much more money going straight than the way you're heading."

"If you think I'm smart, why don't you give me the manager's job. I could do a helluva lot better than the one you've got."

"You probably could, but not with your twisted value system."

Reluctantly I settled for a pittance of what he was asking, rather than litigate with someone who thrived on it. After a friendly chat we shook hands, and a few days later he moved out of my building.

My only regret is that I didn't change him for his next victim. I merely chalked him up as a cost of doing business.

In 1989 I sold my recycled Prospect Mall Shopping Center to three young partners for $1.1 million with $450,000 in cash and subject to a $650,000 mortgage due the following year. But during that year most banks curtailed loans. The new owners were unable to refinance and were threatened with foreclosure. If the bank foreclosed, I would have wound up with the building because I was on the original $650,000 mortgage. Potentially, I could have resold it for $1.1 million and turned their loss into a $450,000 profit.

The bank was willing to extend the mortgage for two years provided *I* guaranteed it.

What to do? Meeting the lender's demand would clutter up my credit line, but if I didn't, the three partners would lose the $450,000 and probably raise a roar of hostility. Do I refuse to guarantee and get the building back with a potential huge profit, or put myself at risk if they mismanage the shopping center and the bank goes after my signature?

I made the right decision. I not only guaranteed the bank's loan, I helped them lease two vacancies that raised their rent roll by $35,000 a year.

In 1992 they got their own mortgage. I was released from my personal obligation, and they now have a good chance of realizing a $200,000 profit on their venture.

By steering my emotions away from greed and by risking for good, I nipped potential ill-will from exploding and spreading. And I gained a fortune of goodwill from the three partners and their hundreds of friends. It was a good deal for them and for me.

Was I a doormat in these three examples and dozens of others? Not at all. Reducing hostility is dynamic action—not the courage of a Gandhi, but the good sense of an ordinary citizen whose evidence of seeing people blow up minor incidents into emotional hurricanes convinced him that such action leads to inferior living.

Hard-hitting businessmen disagree with my leisurely, easygoing way of conducting business. Some facetiously told me they're surprised I didn't wind up in Chapter Eleven.

I've proven the hard-hitting businessmen wrong. My gains from referrals arising out of "turning the other cheek" far outweigh the losses from practicing softball instead of hardball. Besides, it's more fun conducting business in a pleasant goodwill atmosphere than in one charged with emotional turmoil where positive energy is squandered in negative action.

I've often fallen prey to reviewing in my mind what I should have said or am going to say to people who have wronged me, and always it left rivulets of emotional pollutants that rankled me. Thinking negatively can disturb the emotions as much as verbalizing them. When I make that mistake, I turn my mind to some memorable scene and the rankling gradually disappears.

I seldom have to suppress negative thinking because I shy away from situations that cause them. Using prudence to manage my emotions does not inhibit me in any way. On the contrary, it helps them flow smoothly without overflowing or backing up in cul-de-sacs. It's simply good preventative emotional medicine.

DIRECTING THE MIND is more subtle and requires more attention than managing emotions. The mind is where thoughts initiate action—the good and the bad. It can be a searchlight for pro-life, or a sword for anti-life. Confronting the process of thinking are two opposite forces: the busy, human, selfish concerns and the quiet, invisible, spiritual ones. On the mundane surface they appear contrary to each other, like two enemies.

The challenge to thinking is to reconcile the human and spiritual into co-workers, so we can rejoice in their partnership while they reinforce each other.

The mind alone can't meld this ancient duality into harmonious action. It needs the help of the invisible God-Spark. That help is available only to those who seek it.

In addition to meditation, I seek it by watching the overwhelming evidence of how men and women waste their minds and how others elevate them. Their examples are my best teachers.

Joe was a brilliant lawyer and a nationally known bridge player. But these were sidelines. His main interest was operating an illegal odds-making, betting emporium. He was a genius at it, and he bragged one day while I was playing golf with him that he often earned more in one weekend than the average lawyer earns in a year.

"But what if you're caught?" I asked.

"Then I'll use my legal mind to wiggle out."

A year later, he was arrested and jailed for a year, with three years' probation. He came out with a broken ego, disbarment, and a bleak future. By not linking his mind to his God-Spark, he lost his way. His human genius alone was not a dependable guide. He died several years later, a broken man.

Harold was the leading cigarette wholesaler in his city.

"Look," I said when I visited him, "you've made a lot of money. Why continue selling cigarettes when you know it's killing people."

"They haven't proven it yet."

"Twenty-five years ago you could have said that. Not today, and you know it."

"And give up a $200,000-a-year profit?"

"But you're already worth a couple of million. Aren't you bothered that indirectly you're sentencing people to death?"

"You're too idealistic . . . not practical."

I smiled and dropped the subject.

Kevin was a pioneer in the furniture business. When I negotiated a lease with him for a 100,000-square-foot building, I realized how much smarter he was than I. When he sold his business for several million dollars, he invested his money in real estate and doubled it. Then, using his razor-sharp mind, he got into the stock market, and catapulted himself into a $15 million fortune.

At sixty-five, bored with earning more money, he began marketing himself to young girls. His wife had died, and he went wild with his new freedom. He bought condominiums in Florida, Palm Springs, and Madrid, and advertised for young women to live with him. He showered them with gifts—in the hundreds of thousands of dollars. He carried on this debauchery until 85, when be became sick and died in a nursing home.

Had he used his mind to explore what's beyond success, he and society could have enjoyed the gold of his golden years, not the ashes of his wasted life.

A man I knew in Florida legitimately sold fifty times the amount of whiskey Al Capone sold illegitimately. He became a multimillionaire and a pillar of his community—charitable, suave, and a gushing fountain of economic knowledge. With his business acumen, he could have been successful in many businesses that could have bettered society, but instead he chose to become an instrument for catering to drunks and increasing killings on highways. He normalized an abnormality that kept his mind in a money-making straightjacket. He managed his anti-life business brilliantly, but not his mind's potential.

For every mismanaged mind, however, there are dozens that receive thoughts that prompt pro-life societal action.

Bob was not satisfied with selling auto parts even though he was successful at it. When we walked our dogs in the evening, he told me that he was looking for something to make a more significant contribution to society.

When he lost money in several transactions involving bogus checks, an idea lit up his mind. He would accumulate a list of fake-check writers from businesses and sell protection from them for a fee to retailers. He developed this idea with innovative technological skill and formed the Telecheck Company that now sells check protection internationally. He sold the company for several millions, and is now retired in Hawaii.

I know that Bob's primary motivation for changing his work was to serve mankind. Most of the time our discussions focused on ways to combine the secular with the spiritual. In the exchange, we mutually honed our minds to higher purposes.

Several years ago, I had occasion to look into the mind of a reincarnationist.

"Death is a gateway, not an end," the merry-eyed man was saying. He was a retired, self-educated factory worker. "Look, I'm 84 years old. My body is worn out. Like an old suit of clothes, I'm ready to cast it aside. It has served its purpose— a vehicle for the spark of God within me to convert earthly experience into spiritual wisdom."

"Go on," I prodded.

"My sojourn on earth is almost over. I face death, not with sadness, but with a sense of adventure. The capacities I have developed in this lifetime I'll use in the next. There lies my immortality. What scientists call DNA is merely the chemical information the Monad or Soul projects for our next incarnation. Get it?"

"I get it; but what intrigues me is how you, a factory worker, can be so well informed in such profound conjecturing."

"Some use their minds for accumulating money, power, or what have you. I used mine for accumulating spiritual wisdom. You be the judge which is more worthwhile."

"When I see you bubbling with happiness at your age, I have to decide your way."

Minnie spends five afternoons a week visiting the elderly sick at a Jewish Old Home, even though at 88, she's ten years older than the average age of the patients she visits! She still drives, and she follows world events with avid interest. Because she didn't allow her mind to rust, she's still in the mainstream, while others her age are washed ashore. I know her well. Her mind caught a whiff of the spiritual, and it's managing her mind with greater expertise than what the best of psychiatry could do for her.

I CAN'T MANAGE SPIRITUALITY the way I do my mind. It's not measurable or manageable. Because it's unfathomable, I cannot put it in a denominational mold. Where I used to satisfy my religious duty with mere respectable synagogue attendance, my spiritual commitment demands more: that I convert thoughts into deeds. Religion was undemandingly bland compared to the urgent prodding of my spirituality, where more action takes place quietly on the inside than on the noisy outside.

It took quiet time to internalize the fact that I'm made of Nature's stuff—air, water, and earth—the only difference between me and other living entities being that I'm more evolved than some, and less than others. The same logic persuades me that just as each individualized organ of my body cooperates with all my other organs to keep it functioning, so it makes sense that I should cooperate with all entitites of the universe for my benefit, as well as for all its parts. That's what the wisdom of One Life is all about.

This kind of thinking has convinced me that I receive my life energy from my Cosmic Spark, just as the light in a plugged-in lamp gets its power from an electric-power generator on the outskirts of the city. Because my body is plugged into the Cosmic Power, I rely more on its wisdom to heal me than on medicines, and more on Cosmic Intelligence for clear thinking than intellectual psychology or psychiatry.

Even though I've chosen spirituality over religiosity, I'm still grateful for Judaism's and Christianity's wisdom; tolerant of the humanists, existentialists, and atheists; but wary of cults and gurus. They have their evolutionary agendas, I have mine. After years of searching and sifting, I believe I'm more on the cutting edge of spiritual progress by quietly communicating with God than by participating in the hoopla of religious holidays and then putting God on the back burner for the rest of the year—as I used to do.

I'm convinced that by daily stilling my mind, God's thoughts have a far better chance of reaching and teaching me than if I were constantly on the run. During those still moments, I have time to acknowledge that I've been wonderfully led, and experience the healing effect of expressing gratefulness.

It's intriguingly challenging to live this two-tier existence—tending to the mundane and nuturing the spiritual. It's a stimulating experience to see how each reinforces the other. The prosaic provides the grist to prod me, the spiritual refines it.

I've just begun to fathom the inexhaustible reservoir of insights waiting to be discovered. What makes this thought so inspirationally challenging is that, unlike success, I see no end to it. It will keep me evolving for the rest of this life and endless incarnations to follow. Climbing the no-top-in-sight mountain is so much more exhilarating than settling for ''successfully'' arriving at it. Arriving is contrary to my conviction that life is a never-ending, constant becoming; and, as noted earlier: *the journey is the destiny.*

To prepare for the ascent into spirituality, I'm using a practical plan to help me on my pathless way. It's to write down my thoughts after coming out of quiet time for their clarification and evaluation. I've filled thirty-seven, 100-page notebooks with what I call diary leaves.

Undergirding my business success and experience with the wonders of spirituality was the support of my family. I could not have enjoyed and accomplished what I did without them.

9

THE FAMILY IS THE SEED, ROOTS, AND HARVEST OF A FULFILLING LIFE

When the Family Crumbles,
Civilization Crumbles.

FOR THE HUMAN SPECIES TO CONTINUE TO evolve, the family must be made the seed, roots, and harvest for a fulfilling life. Any deviation is violating the natural order. Different family lifestyles may come and go, but they will not be viable substitutes for the advancement of civilization.

My first exposure to family security was my mother's love —which she gave in full measure. It was protective, possessive, and sacrificial—the ingrained characteristics of a typical Jewish mother's caring. These were different compared to today's psychological theories that children should be given freedom to follow their own instincts. I'm not enough of a psychologist to judge which is more effective in the formative years. What I do know is that I felt secure under her protective wings, coping with the early Russian dangers and the many transformations I had to make in America.

My mother's love and my grandfather's support prepared me to play my role in perpetuating family continuity, without which my quest for spiritual development would not have progressed as it did.

WHEN JESUS ASKED HIS DISCIPLES to leave their families and follow him, he thundered with more authority than the religions I investigated.

I didn't leave my family, but I took enough time away from them to create some problems. It was inevitable: my intensity clashed with their mild interest. But my wife, who was the centerpiece of our family, balanced my centrifugal pull with her centripetal wisdom. She was more aware than I that a life is not complete when outside interests take precedence over familial ones. It can be a good life, she contended, but not a fulfilling one.

When I didn't slack off my secular and spiritual pursuits, my wife began looking into carving a career in collecting and dealing in antiques, for which she has a great talent.

When our seven-year-old son tearfully asked my wife, "Are we so poor that you have to work away from home?" she choked up, scrapped her career plans, and became a full-time mother.

I met her sacrifice by cutting down on my activities and spent more time taking the entire family to evenings of ice skating, weeks of ranching in Arizona, and vacationing in Florida ocean resorts. What little I gave up was more than compensated by the glowing feeling of family solidarity.

This familial cohesiveness drew my wife and me into a closer relationship. My strong interests were in lectures, conferences, and reading. Hers were in family caring, interior decorating, helping me with recycling old buildings to new uses, celebrating birthdays, and maintaining orderly and attractive homes. We respected and joined in each other's interests. She traveled with me to Moral Re-Armament conferences, sat alongside me at the Aspen Institute for Humanistic Studies, and even drove with me over a range of mountains to hear Krishnamurti lecture at Ojai, California. I, in turn, gave up Sunday golf to be home with the family, was always home for dinner, shopped with her for her favorite Chinese export antiques, and bottle-fed our infants when they woke up in the middle of the night.

Her sense of humor is a refreshing antidote to my seriousness. When I asked at one of our country-club parties, "Do you know it's already two o'clock in the morning?" she cajolingly purred, "Tell me when it's three o'clock." I smiled and waited.

Her mind and body refused to age. She weighed 112 pounds when I married her, and after 55 years, she still weighs the same, with a beautiful figure that bridges the then and now. Her desire for courtship and zest for romance only waxed with the years.

Her knack of combining joviality with seriousness (she was an *A* student in high school and college) makes her an interesting and fun partner. She has edited all my published six books and fully understands and supports my spiritual quest.

She's the family guru on nutrition, vitamins, home remedies, and a variety of safety precautions. We dovetail our activities with respect and trust. As she pursues her practical wisdoms against the backdrop of what she knows interests me, I, in turn, support her as she attends to the myriad human needs necessary for family cohesion.

I render to the outside its due, but not too far from the family boundary—a border my wife handles with delicacy, diplomacy, love, and understated fervency. As we accommodate to each other, we acquire each other's wisdom while traveling our individual evolutionary paths. We teach each other lessons; and one of the most important ones is not to win an argument, but rather to dissolve the differences that cause it. We both agree that the winner diminishes the loser.

Our lines of communication are always open—free from the debris of doting on past psychological differences, which my wife and I agree, with Krishnamurti, are the cause of much of humankind's miseries.

TO KNIT FAMILY TOGETHERNESS, I decided early on to develop an individual relationship with each of my three children.

Bonnie, the eldest, was the rebel. When she was eighteen months old, she had already developed a feud with our maid. She would sneak up behind her, loosen the strings of her apron, and run away. Our no-nonsense maid didn't think it was funny and, after many similar incidents, threatened to leave. It took all my salesmanship to have her remain. Bonnie teased her younger sister and brother to tears, and my wife and me to parental frustration. I didn't have the fatherly resources then, so that sending her to bed early only exacerbated her mischievous behavior.

In the sixth grade she ran for president of her class on the slogan "I may be small, but I've got big ideas" and beat her opponent, who is now one of the leading lawyers in Wisconsin. After graduating from the University of Wisconsin, her rebelliousness turned from her siblings to the Establishment. She took a social-worker job in the Welfare Department and stuck it out for three years, even after she was threatened with a gun by a welfare recipient when she told him to "Shape up or no welfare check."

She was arrested, jailed, and released after 24 hours when she chained herself to several others in a civil-rights protest march at the courthouse. Against my wishes she traveled to Russia to take a close look at Communism and, at the risk of being followed, looked up my Russian relatives. She came back disenchanted and confused as to where her priorities lay.

During her years of restlessness, I had long talks with her. This was a time when the psychological vogue was to let the children find their own niche without interference. I didn't agree. My rationale was that if I didn't influence Bonnie, others would.

The core of my influence was to praise her curious mind and social action, but I cautioned that we all need to soften work with spirituality (and I explained my quest). "Otherwise," I warned, "we become intellectually brittle."

"Oh, Dad," she countered, "helping people is the highest form of religion. You know it and so do I."

She not only knows it—she does it, pouring in hundreds of hours of pro-bono work a year.

At 24 she fell in love with a politically conservative successful home-builder and made a radical transformation—from a strong liberal to a mainstream independent. To please him, she became a gourmet cook, an excellent homemaker, and later a devoted mother to her two children. That change led her to become active on the boards of Mount Sinai Hospital, the Zoological Society, the Zoo, the Milwaukee Ballet, Planned Parenthood, the local AIDS chapter, and the Milwaukee Art Museum, where she met bank presidents and CEOs of Milwaukee's leading corporations.

She became known for her intimate home gourmet-dinner parties, and as a prominent community leader. Where at the beginning of her change *I* introduced *her* to well-known people, *she* now introduces *me* at social affairs to people who are far more prominent than the ones I know.

We get along beautifully. I love her very much, and I know she loves me. If I asked for more, I'd be asking too much.

MY YOUNGER DAUGHTER, JUDY, was shy as a child and showed her uneasiness in the company of adults. She complained that my country club was "too fancy," that their sophisticated conversation made her uncomfortable. But she was gregariously comfortable and popular with her peers in high school and college. Her popularity was well deserved. She was kind, friendly, and intelligent (she tested two grades beyond her class) and beautiful (she was chosen the beauty of the week at the University of Wisconsin).

Like Bonnie, she was against the Establishment and for the underdog, but without her sister's activism. She disliked the rich and tried to show it by wearing plain, simple clothes. When she came home after a date, she had her escort drop her off a block from our Lake Drive home because she thought it showed off our wealth. And she told me that if I bought a Cadillac, she would never get into it.

Judy was influenced more by the ideological left at the University than what she learned during three years of Jewish Sunday School. That's why, I supposed, she bashed the haves and favored the have-nots. I tried to give her a balanced view.

"Judy, please listen carefully. When you condemn wealth, you condemn me, who have given you a comfortable home and a good education. Character is more important than ideology of left or right, and you can find it among the poor *and* the rich. You're a kind and gentle person, so I can understand your feelings for the underdog—but the rich need understanding too. They need goodwill as much as the poor. *I* need it."

"You have all my goodwill and love as well. But *you're* different. It's the country-club crowd I don't like." Two years after graduation, Judy told us she had chosen to marry a popular, handsome young man of Italian ancestry.

"Will you be able to handle the cultural and religious differences?" we asked.

"There are no differences in love."

But there were. Not the religious and cultural differences, but the temperamental. They didn't mesh. After ten years and two children, their marriage ended in a friendly divorce.

We helped Judy acquire a women's-apparel store, which, with the help of a partner, became the outstanding fashion shop for women in Milwaukee.

Judy's four buying trips a year to New York, work in the store, and our frequent discussions changed her views about the rich. She does not discriminate any more.

She now enjoys waiting on the wives of the millionaire players on the Milwaukee Bucks basketball team, the Milwaukee Brewers, and the Green Bay Packers, who come to her store to buy the latest fashions in women's apparel.

Her shyness with adults and her dislike for the wealthy are long gone. She's become the sophisticated conversationalist she disliked as she was growing up, and now carries herself, as one of the beautiful people of Milwaukee, with poise and confidence.

My spiritual quest appeals only to the few. And Judy—so far—is not yet one of them. But I love her the way she is, and she loves her mother and me with the same devotion as she loves her children.

From my evolution's standpoint, I've learned as much from Judy as she's learned from me.

OVERCOMING IGNORANCE IS MORE IMPORTANT than accumulating knowledge. In the early 1950s, when I saw my ten-year-old son Bobby tinkering in the garage with an old automobile motor, I diminished him with the remark that he was wasting his time. It still gives me a wrenching feeling when I think of it! My accumulated knowledge was not doing me any good.

And while in his teens, when he told me that he'd like to work and maybe live on a Western ranch, rather than be a businessman, I ridiculed the idea. I had not overcome my ignorance with an understanding that he might have been overwhelmed with my success and didn't feel at ease in its shadow.

When he learned to drive, it became his obsession and my concern. When I cautioned him about driving carefully, his response was little more than indifference. I realize now that I had not poured in enough sympathy to his needs to deserve a more positive response.

At nineteen a great change came over him. He fell in love with Mary Carol. His gentle, kind, sensitive nature, which I couldn't reach, she did; and because he found a new happiness, it spilled over into our relationship. I was delighted. We began talking about property management as a starter, and later about other phases of real estate. She did indirectly what I couldn't do directly.

On Father's Day I received a note which I've treasured through the years beyond all others. It read:

> To a wonderful father.
> I hope I didn't
> Cause you too much trouble.
> Just a few lines to let you know
> I really appreciate
> What you are doing for me,
> Although I didn't always show it.
> Love, Bobby

It was simple but, for me, eloquent. I have read and reread it dozens of times, often with tears in my eyes.

My wife and I have never forgotten Mary Carol. She saw in Bobby sensitive qualities I did not fully appreciate. There is an Eastern wisdom which claims that when someone is ready for change, the teacher appears: Bobby was ready when Mary Carol, the teacher, appeared.

When we lost Bobby in an automobile accident, we suffered two tragedies—our beloved son, and the abrupt ending of a beautiful romance.

During the last twenty-five years when our family places flowers on Bobby's grave every October 20th, we always find a beautiful plant left earlier by Mary Carol. She's married now, and apparently to a very fine husband.

Lessons like these can only be learned in the ethos and pathos of family life.

THE SECOND TIER OF MY FAMILY—my four grandchildren—taught me as much with their green experience as I taught them with my maturity.

Andria, 25, Judy's daughter, has been a treasurehouse of grandfatherly and grandmotherly learning. My wife and I watched both from afar and near Andria's burden of her parents' failed marriage. Her grades were only mediocre in grade and high school, even though she tested two grades above her class.

My wife did more than any psychiatrist in easing Andria's mind. Every Saturday she, Judy, and Andria had lunch and shopped the rest of the afternoon. It has become a weekly afternoon of institutionalized happiness.

Every year we invited Judy, Andria, and Bob—Andria's brother, to spend two weeks during the winter at our condominium in Palm Springs, California. I had a golden opportunity to have long talks with the three of them, especially Andria, who I thought needed relief from her worrying mind. I explained that she need not be locked into her parents' problems, that she should take care of her own evolutionary progress (I explained in detail what I meant by this), and that this would free her for a happier outlook on life. During those talks I discovered her superb intelligence.

After an uneventful first year at the University of Wisconsin, Milwaukee, she chose Tempe University in Arizona for her second year because her father had played football there. She contracted some sort of valley fever but stuck it out for an unhappy full year. However, out of the ashes of the lowest point in her life she made a miraculous transformation.

She reentered the University in Milwaukee and became a national honor student. Something even more dramatic happened. She volunteered to take care of two retarded women living in a foster home—feeding, bathing, and entertaining them during her spare time while attending school. As if that pro-bono work wasn't enough, she volunteered to care for abused women two nights a week at a facility located in a dangerous part of town.

What happened? I was seeing a road-to-Damascus transformation right before my eyes—and in my own family! What an exciting experience! But that wasn't the end of surprises. Andria was ready when *her* teacher appeared—a law professor who was so impressed with her legal mind in his international-law class that he convinced her to change her major from psychology to law. She did.

She not only finished her first year of law school with honors, but was chosen to work in the city attorney's office (a great privilege for a first-year law student).

When I asked Andria what branch of law she intends to pursue, she answered without hesitation:

"Public defense. I want to dedicate my life to prosecuting evil and defending good."

Among our many rewards for our patient caring was this note:

> Dear Papa and Nannie:
>
> I want to thank you for everything you've done for me—for being such an important part of my life. I want you to know that even though I tried to close my mind (from Papa) when you talked about wisdom, I've absorbed some of it, and I look forward to absorbing more!
>
> I love both of you very much.
>
> Andria

Change is the most meaningful part of the evolutionary process. Andria glorified it.

BOB, JUDY'S SON, FROM INFANCY on to now, looks and acts just like my son, Bobby. His voice, his mannerisms, his kind, gentle nature are astonishingly similar—except for one difference: our grandson is fiercely enamored of athletics. But it presented a disturbing problem. He was small and light for his age, and it troubled him. Yet, despite his lack of size and weight, at eight he was a star soccer player, outplaying boys a head taller and forty pounds heavier. In one game his team won 7 to 0, and Bob scored all seven points.

To stimulate his growth and weight, he and I worked out a plan where I would weigh and measure him every two weeks, marking the numbers on the wall in our laundry room. When he gained a pound or two, or grew 1/4 inch, we would celebrate by having him drink a rich malted milk. We kept it up until he was 15, when suddenly he exploded into a rapid growth and weight gain so that in his junior year in high school he measured 5'9'' and weighed 140 pounds.

He realized his life-long dream: playing football as his father did when he was an all-state high-school tackle. Bob played on defense, and when I watched him fly through the air with wild abandon to tackle a running back forty pounds heavier than he, I worried more about Bob's getting up, and less about his stopping the runner from scoring.

I edged into his love of sports by teaching him how to play golf (he now outdrives me by 100 yards off the tee). After a game, I would challenge him to an 18-hole putting contest: if *he* won, we would go straight home. If *I* won, he'd have to listen to a fifteen-minute talk on character development (he had no exposure to Jewish or Christian Sunday Schools).

He tried hard to beat me. I tried harder, and usually I'd win. I thinned down what I wanted to say to his level, but not too thin, because he is a very bright young man. The gist of my fifteen-minute sermon was something like this: Please listen to me and not your peers . . . don't experiment with drugs or alcohol, they'll poison your future . . . if you discipline your-self now, you'll be a freer person later . . . practice honesty, it'll help you in business and in all other relationships . . . begin to think how God can play a role in your life . . . I'll explain how in later discussions.

He would listen politely, and when we got in the car, we talked only about golf, football, and other matters.

There hasn't been a time when we didn't hug each other on meeting or saying good-by, either alone or in a crowd.

ROBERT, BONNIE'S 23-YEAR-OLD SON, showed his smart, practical nature early. At four, while I was dragging him up a steep, slippery slope at the edge of my yard leading down to Lake Michigan (it was after a rain), I couldn't get solid footing and we kept slipping back. After four tries, Robert said, "Papa, why don't you try another spot?" I did, and I hauled him up the cliff using a drier area.

And at five, I took Robert along when I was called to assess the flood damage caused by a broken pipe that inundated the lower level of my Prospect Mall with two feet of water. From the first floor I heard one of the owners of the flooded stores scream from below, "If I get that Bockl, I'm going to wring his neck for ruining my business!" Robert turned to me. "Papa, I think we'd better leave." I took his advice and left.

He is as charming as he is smart, and it flowered during his student days at Tucson University, Arizona, where he matured into a clean-cut, disciplined, well-mannered young man. With his 3.2 average in real estate and finance, I had to be on my toes defending my views against his ultraconservative ones when he came home during vacations, and in long and frequent tele-phone talks.

He has all the qualities to become a successful real-estate entrepreneur and the ambition to get there. His goal is well defined, but not the means. In our discussions, he never mentioned any elevating thoughts from his teachers nor any wisdom from his two years of Jewish Sunday School. I tried to fill the gap.

"Robert," I said one afternoon when we sat down in my study, "let's review the serious part of what I've been writing to you at school. Because you have so much going for you, I don't want you to spoil it with the rat-race philosophy that's so prevalent today. Business is not a game, and winning is not its name. Business is a means to make a contribution to society. It may sound corny, but with that attitude you'll enjoy a triple win: you'll help people, make a profit, and enjoy the happiness that produces both.

"Remember what I often told you: building a good reputation is more important than building a huge fortune . . . and developing a giving rather than a grasping nature will bring you more glowing rewards than piling up millions. I don't want to pour cold water on your ambition, but in my view you'd be a failure if you succeeded to become a ruthless real-estate tycoon. Follow your father's ethical standards—that's why he has a reputation as one of the outstanding home builders in the city. I'll watch you from the sidelines, with an assist whenever you need it."

He listened politely. When I finished, he said:

"Papa, you're asking me to aim too high. I'll try. How much I'll reach, I don't know."

I smiled and looked at the eager, handsome young man who has a world of wisdom waiting to be discovered.

After our discussion, we got up, hugged each other, and said "I love you" at the same time. And he left.

      ⭩   ⭩   ⭩   ⭩   ⭩

JORDANA, 21, IS ROBERT'S YOUNGER SISTER, and the Scarlett O'Hara of my grandchildren. One of her pieces of devil-may-care impetuousness is to drive in her bright yellow covertible with the wind blowing through her long hair. But while she seems ethereal, she's got her feet on the ground—breezing through her four years of college with a B + average.

Jordana's an adventurer. She took one college semester of school on a ship that took her around the globe—with two extra trips from her ship by airplane to Singapore and China. A year later she signed up for a year of study in Paris, at the American University. While there she traveled alone by train to Italy, Hungary, Belgium, and the Netherlands. At home during the summer vacation, she parked cars, worked as a waitress, and helped her mother with her volunteer AIDS work. My wife has lunch with her on Saturdays, usually in the company of Andria and Judy, and they have a hilarious shopping time afterward, Jordana prodding my wife toward "get-with-it" fashions, and my wife restraining her way-out, modish ideas.

Though she's always on the move, I've managed to reach her with my letters while she sailed around the world, in Paris, and at home. She's a delight to talk with, because she's a truly cultivated person—majoring in art with minors in the Western mind and international affairs. She knows more about Gorbachev, Bergson, Bacon, and Camus than I do, and I'm a neophyte compared to her knowledge of Indian, Greek, French, and American art.

One day she complained that I was giving serious advice to her brother and neglecting her. I was surprised! Heretofore, I had met her vivaciousness with conversational levity.

"Are you really interested?" I asked.

"Of course! Don't you think I need wisdom?

I grasped at the chance because I had many things to tell her. First, she was taking too many chances in these dangerous times, especially her spirited driving in the yellow convertible. She agreed to be more careful. I explained my search beyond success just to get her reaction to something totally new to her. Her beautiful, angelic face turned pensive as she pried me with cogent questions. Surprised at her perceptiveness, I went further and explained the four prerequisites for a value building life—Meditation, Evaluation, Transformation, and Implementation.

"That's great, Papa!" she exclaimed.

Now that I had her attention, I ventured further.

"You know, Jordana, those who fly high have to be careful not to plummet. The best place to live in a home is in the living room, not in the basement or attic. The restless high flyers have to be extra careful not to end below or on top of the living room."

"Papa, I suppose you're afraid I might not only wind up in the attic, but go through the roof."

I smiled, and she patted me on the back.

"Don't worry, that'll never happen to your granddaughter. But thank you so much for caring. I know what you're driving at. I'm so lucky. I have the most wonderful grandparents in the world. I just love you and Nannie!"

I opened a spigot of understanding I didn't know was there. She indeed had her feet on the ground, and my admiration for her took a quantum leap.

She has two wonderful parents, but I assured her that should she want extra love and attention, her grandparents would always be there at a moment's notice.

 🧍 　 🧍 　 🧍 　 🧍 　 🧍

AFTER MY ACTIVE INVOLVEMENT with my family, business, and what's beyond success, I end with the most ultimate question: What's the nature of our immortality? It's at the heart of all religions and beyond. What does it really mean? I venture this conjecture, looking into a small opening of vast unfathomables:

Just as giving anonymously is the highest and most unselfish form of giving, so could it not be that pouring in the most elevating pro-life activity during our incarnation, without knowing the identity of who's going to inherit it, is a wiser view of immortality than the more selfish view of wanting to identify our continuity with the person who is going to benefit from our progress, or the even more selfish view of wanting to live forever in bliss in some heavenly location?

This view poses two intriguing questions: What kind of a person passed on his or her progress to me? and What kind of man or woman will inherit mine?

Based on my present knowlcdge, I'll never know. But what if the small opening grows wider, and I see and understand more? That's the challenge that will keep me on the timeless, trackless, never-ending evolutionary journey.